Black American History

A Comprehensive Guide to 400 Years of African American History, Systemic Challenges, and Group Survival

DC Cannon

Contents

Special Acknowledgement

This book was penned during the George Floyd fallout, and under the looming threat of anticipated book bans for works of this nature. Its intended audience is clearly Black Americans and the conscious community, with little consideration for others. There are a few demographics that have surprisingly responded positively to this book, and I would like to give a sincere thanks to each group separately in this acknowledgement.

The author has long concluded that the stewards of white supremacy have been attempting to eradicate Blacks for centuries, and believes it imperative to document such efforts in a book before it is too late. Therefore, this so-called "history" book deviates from the norm; unlike any other history book, this one contends that in the final analysis, Black American history substantiates claims of systematic genocide perpetrated to maintain white domination. Originally intended for distribution in barbershops, activists, community centers, the man-on-the-street, and independent Black bookstores, with the internet and the general public as an afterthought, the author never anticipated such widespread interest in this kind of book. Surprisingly, individuals of various backgrounds, including Japan, Australia, China, Italy, Mexico, the UK, and beyond, have embraced this book. Particularly heartening is the overwhelming response from white society and the same-sex community, which has deeply touched the author. I extend my deepest appreciation to all who have approached my book on racism and white domination with an open heart and mind.

My books are well-written, hardcore, and intentionally crafted to convey raw, unvarnished truths regarding white supremacy and without any sugar-coating. Readers should know that well over a dozen individuals—most of them white, dedicated themselves tirelessly to bring my books to fruition. Among numerous editors, several layout personnel, countless cover designers, and a few book coaches, both men and women—not a single individual involved in this project has raised complaints, taken personal offense, or misconstrued my message as an accusation against all white people as being racist. I am immensely grateful for the guidance and expertise of my coach, Karina (a Jew from Poland), my layout specialist, Nadine (American), and my editor, Renae (Australian). These invaluable professionals—all white women, who have tirelessly dedicated themselves to this book while offering valuable suggestions, and never took any of the contents of this book personally.

The author is a big fan of the late, great Dr. Amos Wilson and Malcolm X, admires the Black Panthers, and resonates with many of Minister Louis Farrakhan's teachings. Yet, in working with this team of dedicated professionals I have never felt the need to justify or hesitate to state anything, and before, during, and after the production not a single objection has arisen to the content within these pages. This level of tolerance and understanding has evoked warm and respectful feelings within the author, suggesting that some white individuals and white society as a whole may possess a greater depth of sophistication than initially presumed.

It was surprising to find that so many white people not only want to read a book that condemns white domination and connects Black history with genocide, but also showed empathy and understanding towards its message and the plight of Black people. Your grasp of the complexities of racial dynamics and your readiness to confront uncomfortable truths have been truly appreciated. Your empathy and solidarity shine as beacons of hope in our collective pursuit of a fairer and more equitable society. I am deeply moved by your capacity to understand that discussions about racism do not implicate every white individual, but rather illuminate systemic injustices that are used to maintain domination. Whether we accept it or not, Black people have been dominated by another group for centuries. This subjugation inevitably breeds certain beliefs and sentiments rooted in the harsh realities of oppression. This book embodies the sentiments born out of the routine experiences endured by members of the oppressed group. Many of these expressions are vividly articulated within the pages of this book.

Acknowledging that allies can arise from diverse backgrounds is not entirely new; the author's upbringing and experiences have immersed him in various environments. Furthermore, many of us have witnessed individuals, irrespective of ethnicity and including white people, courageously advocating for racial equality. From kneeling in solidarity and participating in fervent debates alongside Black peers, to enduring lengthy voting lines to oppose openly racist politicians, individuals from various walks of life have stood together in the fight for racial justice. The author's contention lies not with all white people—it is with white supremacy, paternalism, and the systemic racism that perpetuates domination and culminates into systematic population control.

Your willingness to listen, learn, and empathize speaks volumes about your character as individuals, white society as a whole, as well as your personal commitment to equality and justice. Your understanding paves the way for meaningful dialogue and transformative change.

In addition, some members of the same-sex community surprised me in their maturity in dealing with positions that are contrary to their own. I am deeply grateful for the readers who engaged with my book, even though it may have caused discomfort or disagreement. Your willingness to read and consider differing perspectives, even when they challenge your own beliefs, demonstrates a remarkable level of openness and maturity the author never knew existed. I want to express my sincere appreciation for your support and class throughout this process. If you are offended by this book but read it anyway, the author feels indebted and owes you his undivided attention in return.

Your willingness to engage in dialogue and understanding, despite any differences in opinion, is truly commendable. Thank you for your thoughtful engagement and for contributing to the broader conversation on important social issues. Due to the stand taken in this book, some members of the alphabet community will take issue with some of my stated positions and still require some reassurance. Therefore, I want to address some of the concerns that will likely emerge regarding my stance on gay rights, and white power using sexuality to sustain domination. While I understand that my views may not align with everyone's beliefs, those views are not driven by bigotry. Advocating for traditional values and expressing reservations about certain aspects of the gay rights movement does not stem from a place of hatred or discrimination.

Like any normal and decent person, if I witnessed someone assaulting an innocent person because of their lifestyle, I would object to the attack, render aid if needed, and testify in court if given the opportunity. If a lesbian couple applied to rent my apartment and met the qualifications, I would rent to them without hesitation. Similarly, if a homosexual applied for a job, even at my own company, and met the qualifications, he would stand a fair chance of being employed.

My concern is not directed at individuals personally or what consenting adults do behind closed doors; rather, it is with a faction within white society that has taken it upon themselves to destroy the traditional values once prevalent in Black America, dismantling longstanding culture, and promoting contrary behavior beyond its organic existence. Leftist white power has specifically singled out Blacks, making them the face of all things queer. Right or wrong, many in the Black community suspect that white power is popularizing homosexuality in the community in order to reduce the size of the population. The author shares this belief, and is unapologetically angered by this sinister, systematic effort and the purpose behind it. But that does not mean that I am not able to treat individuals with the same respect that I expect in return. Opposing white domination does not mean opposing all Caucasians, and opposing another group popularizing a lifestyle to fulfill an agenda does not mean opposing all individuals who personally engage in the lifestyle.

To better understand why so many Blacks around the world reject efforts to popularize a chosen sexuality in the group, one must study the practice known as "cultural colonization," which involves replacing existing behaviors with those of another group to maintain influence and secure control. (Cultural colonization is explored further in chapter two) It raises suspicion when America and Europe sanction African nations for refusing to embrace the same-sex agenda, yet does not apply the same pressure to Arab or Asian countries that reject homosexuality and gay rights. Why doesn't white American power strive to transform Asian and Latin American societies and rid them of homophobia as they did with Black Americans? Calling attention to this disparity, or objecting to it, is not about hate; it warrants an explanation beyond mere name-calling. Anyone calling the author a homophobic, or anti-Semitic, or racist, is not basing that on facts or from any firsthand knowledge or experience. As said on the streets, "No matter who you are, if you are cool with me, I am cool with you."

It is crucial to recognize that disagreement with certain elements of the gay rights movement does not always equate to intolerance or bigotry. It can be a matter of personal belief, cultural upbringing, opposition to a weaponizing sexuality to fulfill an agenda, and sometimes religious conviction. The intention is not to spread animosity or division, but rather to engage in respectful dialogue about complex social issues.

Furthermore, I want to emphasize that respect and empathy for individuals regardless of lifestyles or sexual preferences are fundamental principles that guide my interactions with others. While we may hold differing opinions, it is imperative that we treat one another with kindness and understanding. We are all in this together; let us continue to engage in conversations that foster understanding and bridge divides, even when our perspectives differ. Thank you for your attention and willingness to engage with challenging topics.

Finally, I am incredibly impressed and deeply grateful for the overwhelming support from the Black community in response to this book. I totally underestimated the number of Black readers out there. I never anticipated such a large number of Black people who both buy books and read them, and your enthusiasm has truly exceeded my expectations. Your engagement with the book and your willingness to explore its themes and messages mean the world to me. Thank you for embracing my work and for your unwavering support. Your presence and participation in this journey have made a profound impact, and I am sincerely grateful for your support and encouragement. I find your eagerness to read this book to be both shocking and pleasant.

May this special acknowledgement convey appreciation and gratitude to both proponents and opponents who engage thoughtfully with discussions on racism and equality.

BLACK AMERICAN HISTORY

Introduction

The rise of Europeans and white power has had a devastating impact on Black societies all over the world. White power's torrent of racial oppression and hatred is responsible for a 450 year Black Holocaust far worse than the 12 year holocaust associated with white Jews. The sad truth is that white society has been controlling and depopulating Black people for so long that the blatant effort and end results have been normalized. The Black community has become numb and even casual regarding a centuries old genocide that has gained momentum and— verifiably stunted the growth of Black America.

This book uses historical facts and day-to-day racism as proof of both diabolical and subtle efforts used by white functionaries of racial destruction to control and kill Black people. *Black American History* intends to demonstrate that a three dimensional effort to depopulate Black people is now in full effect with stunning results. Historically, white hegemony has used instrumental genocide worldwide to establish the current socio-economic racial hierarchy, and today, white power uses a variety of means to control Black wealth, leadership, birthrate and lifespan. *Black American History* examines white society's endless effort to control and systematically cull Black people, leaving most readers to conclude that the indisputable goal is obviously extermination.

Whenever racism is indicated, one typical response is to advise someone to "stop victimizing." To tell Blacks not to victimize is preposterous and just a way to normalize racial mistreatment. White society still cannot quite "get over" OJ Simpson being acquitted but have the nerve to tell people who are experiencing an ongoing holocaust to "get over it." This victimization charge is just another way to avoid hearing any gripes about racism. These people want to ignore the existence of racism and thereby standardize it along with locking in the advantages it brings white society. Here is a fair question. Black civilization has dealt with over 350 years of slavery, and another 150 years of systematic abuse after slavery ended—at what point can this history be discussed? To put it bluntly, white power has done so much harm to Black society that it is not humanly possible to chronicle all of it inside a single book.

The historical calamities heaped upon humanity by Europeans are so substantial that a team of professionals would have to commit to several decades of work in order to produce the full scope of the ruin. Chronicling the adverse effects of grappling with a 500-year-old racial system of hate would produce a volume of work so gigantic that it would set a permanent record for the largest encyclopedia ever written. This book has omitted far too much mistreatment to be about victimization, and in fact by limiting inserts to actions intended to either control or decimate Blacks allowed the author to exclude all other hateful acts of oppression.

While avoiding victimization, *Black American History* instead focuses on inventorying an assortment of controlling tactics and deadly weapons used by the white ruling class against the subjugated Black masses. It must be noted that while writing this book there were countless media reports of white power advocates and systems killing Black people. Ahmaud Aubery was shot by racists while jogging. A gruesome ten minute recording exposed a Minneapolis cop kneeing George Floyd to death, setting off months of mass protest. Sean Reed recorded Indianapolis police shooting him 10 times in the back and then joking about a closed casket funeral. Breonna Taylor was murdered after police broke into the wrong home and shot her numerous times. It was quite difficult researching and writing a book of this nature while white power crusaders simultaneously murdered Black people. While researching the various ways that white supremacy has historically killed Blacks in the *past*, countless race-based murders *today* served as a reminder that devotees to white power are as hateful and lethal today as ever.

In *Black American History,* readers will find the featured tactics and weapons systems used to control and slowly annihilate Black people include: Chattel slavery, convict labor leasing, sharecropping, Jim Crow, benign neglect, mass incarceration, predatory lending, assassinating or exiling Black leaders, Tuskegee Experiment, violent cops, emasculating black men, red-lining, using drugs and liquor, financing violent rap used to promote self-hatred, gang activity and destroying Black image. Massive or widespread birth control schemes such as abortion are explained and readers will learn how forcing same-sex lifestyles onto a minority group violate several tenets of the United Nation's definition of genocide.

Simply put, *Black American History* will demonstrate that every standardized weapon in the racist toolbox seeks to completely control, outright eliminate or control and eliminate Black people all over the world. Supremacist strategists realize the more pathology they can instill in the Black community the easier it is to justify any form of mistreatment. While *Black American History* encompasses many abusive weapons it must be emphasized that no small book can chronicle all efforts to eradicate Blacks, and yet even an abbreviated overview reflects genuine holocaust. In *Black American History* white society's well-polished resume is reevaluated due to a synopsis factually rooted in undeniable Black Genocide. While a civilized and whitewashed resume has been presented to the world causing the deification of all things white, here's the real *Black American History* and an accurate accounting of the deadly weapons systems and controlling tactics used by white supremacy. Now without further ado, introducing the real *Black American History.*

BLACK AMERICAN HISTORY

Chapter One:
How White Supremacy *Controls* Black Americans

This chapter will focus on the many diverse weapons systems and stratagems utilized by white power to exert control over Black progress and populations.

What: Cultivating Sellouts, AKA "Uncle Toms"

When: 1400s to Present

How: By Offering Money, Jobs and Acceptance

Why: To Advance Racist Interests and Provide Cover for Naked Aggression, Racism and Genocide in order to Control the Black Masses

Who: Partnership between Self-Hating Blacks and White Racists

Category: Dissident Control, Divide and Conquer

Status: In Full Effect, Alert Level-CONDITION-RED

Using black infidels to help manage the masses is essential to the interests of white supremacy, and pre-dates any other weapon to control Black economics and independence. It is befitting to begin with discussing Uncle Toms because this particular weapon is as old as the relationship between Blacks and Caucasians, as sell-outs were used to facilitate the African slave trade hundreds of years ago. *The American Directory of Certified Uncle Toms* is a factual and incredibly well written book that is nothing short of a masterpiece. There is nothing that has been said or written on the subject that it does not cover and explain with stunning clarity. On page 11 the very first paragraph of the book says it all:

> There is no more a detestable trait bred into the Black slave in America then that which compels him to sell out his own Black people. Throughout the ages, the Black race has encountered among its own a species of race traitor ever willing to aid and abet the universal cause of white supremacy. From the Africans who assisted the European slave traders, to the plantation house niggers who dutifully protected their masters' racist regime, blacks could be counted among those who aided in the nearly 500-year-old race war of annihilation now known as the Black Holocaust.[1]

During the darkest times of history when his brethren were treated like beasts of burden, these prized black agents took up arms for the confederacy, double-crossed freedom seeking slaves by betraying slave revolts, apprehended and returned escapees, aided in the sale of the enslaved, justified being in bondage and counseled devotion to their open enemies. They even routinely defended their sadistic captors with their lives. In modern times they are used to endorse racist policies, blame the victims of racism and defend racists, acquit or rationalize police brutality, serve as professional-excuse-makers and reinforce fanatical views expressed by rabid extremists, provide racial discord, root for racists during debates, deny systemic racism or white privilege exists, exuberantly oppose reparations, criticize complaining and protesting, scuttle any plans for an independent project or school, object to a favorable grassroots political campaign, come out swinging against homegrown economic initiatives or derail Black community efforts intended to secure a greater degree of group autonomy. These black-faced white supremacists are the first to claim "victimization" anytime someone briefly discusses unpleasant Black history which incriminates racists. By supporting white supremacy they support the decimation of Black civilization and, realistically only an anomaly of mankind would oppose reparations and obstruct desperately needed racial cohesion—choosing instead to aggressively back an enemy group's effort to expunge their own kind from the Earth.

An expert at propagating rumors and disseminating disinformation to impede Black economic security, never does the hired bootlicker display any unique critical thinking or originate effective ways to establish commercial business centers to economically uplift the Black community. Rarely does the black sell-out who exclusively criticizes Blacks ever positively impact the Black community with their rhetoric and point to a contingent of upwardly mobile Black people saved from poverty due to their influence. To the contrary these self-hating black impediments are hired to contain the masses and repudiate strong Black leadership in his master's exact words and for this service the Uncle Tom is a sought after spokesperson or responsible leader. This describes the *traditional* Uncle Tom who has been used by far-right race soldiers for centuries.

Likewise, white liberals have always used a cadre of handpicked negro proxies to serve as appointed fiduciaries to manage Black political, fiscal and sociological concerns. Not to be outdone by the far-right, the elite leftist white rulers also employ despicable sycophants to serve as surrogates in fulfilling their inimical self-serving agendas and bolster detrimental beliefs about the Black man. For example, some leftist negro flunkies unhesitatingly reinforce negative stereotypes by gladly accepting a range of abominable roles in Hollywood films and commercials. Showing little regard for any Black agenda, black liberal lackeys aided the Democratic Party in establishing "benign neglect" by fervently supporting distractive interests—effectively drowning out Black group concerns. Far-left controllers utilize anonymous black figureheads to give white-owned organizations like the NAACP legitimacy and guide the liberation movement away from self-reliance and into white dependency. Usually the first time the Black population ever heard of these unknown "leaders" is when white power introduced them on television news programs.

Black liberals have no qualms campaigning for useless alien agendas that aren't indigenous and are antithetical to Black interests. For instance, even though a particular lifestyle is infamously rife with diseases like AIDS and strategically lowers birthrate, countless black liberals traitorously took the lead in destroying the Black traditional family by diligently lobbying for and fully supporting gay rights. Apparently they care more about white reward and acceptance than an AIDS epidemic or a shortened lifespan and a reduced birthrate (genocide). Rarely do *hundreds* of Blacks take to the streets to protest on behalf of Black causes while *millions* of them demonstrate annually for homosexual concerns. To understand how erroneous this is one should know that demographically homosexuals have the highest median income in the United States and there isn't a single "gay ghetto" in the world. Population control measures rooted in dangerous lifestyles are enemy constructs that don't offer a single benefit to Black interest one iota yet is highly regarded in most black liberal circles. Some Uncle Toms claim to be *heterosexuals* but are actually willing to die in a fistfight against an opponent of gay rights.

"Progressive" blacks are well aware that sterility clinics are placed in white areas and abortion clinics are placed in Black sections, but the value of white praise far outweighs killing thus far 20 million Black babies and counting. Even though the Black community is seeking reparations and suffering from urban renewal schemes, rogue police, mass incarceration, violent hate groups, lead-poisoning, negative Hollywood stereotypes, poor academic performance, black-on-black crime, drug addiction, discrimination in the workplace, gun violence, poverty, tenanted dilapidated housing, absentee fathers and so much more, almost all black liberals single out just one or two of these concerns and then devote the rest of their time lobbying for irrelevant alternative issues given to them by white left-wing elites. Black liberals must reconsider embracing any construct offered by any group that has a historically well-deserved reputation of loathing and mistreating Blacks. Both *Black American History* and the real world white resume suggest that Blacks proceed with extreme caution regarding socio-economic proposals, political agendas and road maps offered by white society.

Anytime anyone sees a black American marching for illegal immigration, gay rights, animal rights, feminism or the environment they are looking at a person serving white leftist interests without any requirements, alliance or reciprocal support from the groups they campaign for. The reason why homosexuals only protest for gay rights and feminists only work on feminist issues is because they intelligently realize their challenges require exclusive attention by members of the group. The average misguided black liberal who takes to the streets rarely does so for Black causes, so obviously they care less about overall Black plight than they do about appeasing the white power structure.

Black Americans are living behind enemy lines and remain in crisis freefall, in literal need of an all-hands-on-deck approach to solving a myriad of deeply rooted problems transmitted by white power. Any Black activist undividedly dedicated to those issues wouldn't have enough time or energy to protest for others.

Black turncoats have no bounds and have even been known to serve the U.S. government as official informants against freedom seeking Black organizations. In 1969, a time when the most basic human and civil right was a mere fantasy the FBI commissioned an Uncle Tom to infiltrate the Black Panthers in what is believed to be a COINTELPRO operation. While that alone wasn't anything new this particular time informant William O'Neal was instructed to draw a map of the apartment indicating where leader Fred Hampton slept and then slip Hampton a sedative so he would sleep right through his own assassination. Chicago police discharged their weapons over 100 times to guarantee his murder.

Throughout history there have always been black operatives willing to perform any hurtful task asked of them in exchange for money, employment or provisions. From 1967 to 1972 an FBI program called The Ghetto Informant Program (GIP) was able to easily recruit over 7,400 black defectors to help wreck Black organizations and spy on top leadership. Targets included Martin Luther King, Malcolm X, Elijah Muhammad and many other notable leaders along with the corner bakery, barber shops, church and local shoe store. The stated goal was to establish "listening posts" by recruiting people who "live or works in a ghetto area" to provide information "regarding the racial situation" and "racial activities." These black Judases received specific assignments, spied, attended rallies and meetings held by Black leaders as well as informed on the movements and whereabouts of freedom fighters.[2]

Eventually the GIP was investigated and here is how one committee assessed the scale of the FBI and other intelligence groups' attacks on Blacks:

> "The tactics used against [Black] Americans often risked and sometimes caused serious emotional, economic or physical damage. Actions were taken which were designed to break up marriages, terminate funding or employment, and encourage game warfare between rival groups." [3]

The former head of the domestic intelligence division described counterintelligence as "rough, tough, dirty, and dangerous work.[4] One thing that should be pointed out is the GIP ran alongside its much bigger sister COINTELPRO. It is also worth noting that these freedom seeking organizations were considered by the FBI to be "extremists" when actually they were only seeking basic rights such as a right to vote, fair housing or eating inside a café. In other words there were thousands of black data collectors and double-agents who enthusiastically provided intelligence to counteract legal efforts to secure equality and basic rights such as sufficient employment. White hegemony has never harmed Blacks without the help of other blacks. Given the fascination and insecurities that white society has regarding Black people, overt and covert operations of intelligence gathering for the purpose of controlling Blacks and thwarting any freedom struggles remain in full effect to this day.

What: Jim Crow

When: 1890 to 1965

How: By Passing Restrictive Laws Establishing Judicial Decree, Enforced by Law Enforcement

Why: An Inability to Accept Freedom and a Refusal to See Black People as Human Beings, Instead Imposing Economic Lockout in Order to Prevent Upward Mobility While Treating Them Like Animals.

Who: The U.S. Government, Enforced by Police and the General Public

Category: Wealth Prevention

Status: Inactive, Reverberating

This will be the last time you see Jim Crow in respective caps (with lowercase jim crow to signify respect withheld). Originally, in 1828 jim crow was the name of a minstrel routine performed by Thomas Dartmouth Rice and other imitators. In 1890 the court ruled that racial separation was legal as long as the facilities were "separate but equal." The facilities were rarely equal and eventually the term jim crow came to define the overall system of segregation. Many aspects of life was segregated such as drinking fountains, bathrooms, telephones, entrances, housing, parks, swimming pools, jobs, beaches, schools, hospitals, nursing homes and even the cemetery. During the jim crow era mundane actions like eating inside a restaurant, moving into certain areas, riding in the front of the bus or attempting to vote could be lethal for Black people.[5]

What: Benign Neglect

When: 1970s to Today

How: By Lumping Lesser Aggrieved Groups with Blacks and Using Plural Speech When Addressing Black Concerns

Why: To Drown Out Black Voices and Ignore Black Concerns

Who: White Politicians, Leftist Uncle Toms

Category: Diluting Political Power

Status: Active

Don't let the word "benign" fool you, one dictionary defines benign neglect as "an attitude or policy of ignoring an often delicate or undesirable situation that one is held to be responsible for dealing with." For over 50 years major political parties in the United States has employed this strategy in order to subordinate the Black community.

Vague terms like "disadvantaged," "minority," "people of color," and "inner city" are used to prevent directly confronting Black issues and offering specific assistance or racial justice. During jim crow segregation there were ubiquitous signs stating "Whites only" and

"Blacks only." Anyone who wasn't white or Black were not usually relegated to Black facilities but instead given access to the same amenities as white society. Interestingly, with few exceptions Latinos, Asians and others were normally allowed access to the same amenities as white society and NOT categorized with Blacks. In the military they were placed inside segregated "white only" barracks with white soldiers. In "white only" theaters and restaurants they ordinarily sat beside white people. They drank out of "white only" water faucets. But decades later when Blacks pressed for equality suddenly these same groups were placed alongside Blacks and even given priority as though they were mistreated the same as the Black population.

How bad is benign neglect? Countless authors use terms like "people of color" or "minorities" when writing about slavery instead of keeping the discussion accurately on Black Americans. The Democratic Party enjoys about 92 percent of the Black vote which accounts for about 40 percent of the overall democratic vote, yet Black voters watch the Democratic Party fight harder for illegal immigrants than their critical Black constituencies. Thanks to benign neglect that crucial Black vote hasn't enjoyed a hard promise exclusively to Black people since the 1960s. How did benign neglect become a reality? After murdering, exiling, threatening and imprisoning vital leadership of the 1960s white power took it a step further by co-opting elite Black leaders and transformed them into "utility leaders."

Once they pledged loyalty to major political parties Black leadership became known as champions of ALL causes, fighting for ALL people, ultimately abandoning Black causes. Suddenly "Black" leaders battling exclusively for Black causes became strictly prohibited. Literally everyone else became valued constituents and seemingly much more coveted than Black people. Everyone else includes but is not limited to feminists, Latinos, environmentalists, Asians, white women and even illegal immigrants who can't legally vote. Whenever anyone hears a statement about Blacks the next thing they hear is all-inclusive speech that includes almost the entire list mentioned above, as though they can't limit their conversation to only Blacks. For example, let's suppose a particular Black neighborhood is having a problem with speeding traffic and a dozen stop signs are needed.

The system of benign neglect disallows the conversation from focusing only on the Black neighborhood and instead it requires the discussion to extend to others who aren't experiencing the same problem. Instead of saying "we need to get this Black neighborhood the stop signs needed to curb speeding," the language is more like "we need to help Latinos, Asians and women get the stop signs needed to curb speeding." That lessens the attention given to Blacks and redirects stop signs to areas where they are not needed, resulting in only allocating a select few to Black areas. Groups lumped in with Blacks are double-dipping; they enjoy exclusive political attention and they are included in resources aimed at Blacks.

Another end result of benign neglect is the same-sex movement became the permanent darling of the Democratic Party with Blacks relegated to the periphery, done at a time the democrats needed the Black vote and were also able to get elected without the same-sex community. To counteract benign neglect the Black community must strongly oppose other groups consistently placed alongside them and reject vague and indirect jargon and instead insist on specific speech with tangible promises from the political establishment, period.[6]

What: Red-Lining, Urban Renewal and Lending Schemes

When: 1934 to Present

How: By Using Construction Projects and Lending Regulations to Obstruct Homeownership and Real Estate Wealth

Why: To Deny Home Equity and Guarantee Financial Inequality by Relegating Blacks to a Tenant Class, Helping to Assign a Badge of Inferiority to Black Skin

Who: Government Agency, Factions of White Conspirators and Co- Conspirators

Category: Black Wealth Prevention

Status: In Effect

Today people see the geographical location of Black neighborhoods and never question why many live specifically in the big cities or in ghettos. The role that violence played is highlighted in the section that discusses the lynching used to establish sundown towns. In this section the role that institutional racism played in granting home loans is examined. For centuries the oppressor race has used everything from violence to politics to undermine Black homeownership and impede financial success. From 1825 to 1857 New York's Seneca Village was a prosperous predominately Black enclave until jealous whites used "eminent domain" to raze it in order to build Central Park.[7] Fast-forward 100 years and big cities greeted incoming Blacks with state-sponsored systems of segregation implemented through predatory lending practices. In 1934 the U.S. Government established the FHA which was complicit in providing affordable housing to the white middle-class and lower-class, while redirecting the Black masses into housing projects and ghettos. The FHA simply refused to insure any property owned by Black citizens or located near Black areas because they reasoned that any property located near them would automatically decline in value.[8]

The FHA had no basis for this conclusion and in fact on the rare occasion that Blacks did purchase a home in an all-white area the property values increased because they often paid more for the home than whites did. The rationale the FHA used was based purely on racism and not on any scientific study or patterns. The federal government created maps of every metropolitan area in the country and Black populations were denoted with a red line in order to designate those areas as undesirable. The redline maps served as templates to determine what areas to avoid lending money, insuring mortgages or making investments. The FHA also disallowed selling homes to Black buyers. Eventually these color-coded maps were adopted by the Veterans Administration and all proximities near Black Americans were colored red to indicate to appraisers that these neighborhoods were too risky to insure mortgages. Richard Rothstein, author of *The Color of Law* points out these decades-old housing policies have had a lasting effect on American society.

> "The segregation of our metropolitan areas today leads ... to stagnant inequality, because families are much less able to be upwardly mobile when they're living in segregated neighborhoods where opportunity is absent," he says. "If we want greater equality in this society, if we want a lowering of the hostility between police and young African-American men, we need to take steps to desegregate."[9]

For clarity on their segregation policies the FHA wrote the *Underwriting Manual*, which stated "incompatible racial groups should not be permitted to live in the same communities." This meant no lending or selling to Black people allowed. This blatant discrimination was not a matter of law but it was a matter of government regulation. In a system dedicated to precluding Black prosperity the guidelines written in the *Underwriting Manual* demonstrate just one of many crucial roles the U.S. Government played in creating everlasting Black poverty.[10] Predatory lending in Baltimore alone costs Black homeowners almost 4 billion dollars in home equity causing residents to file a massive class-action lawsuit. The formula used in Baltimore and elsewhere involved white land developers and realtors approaching white homeowners and scaring them with false claims of Blacks flocking to their white-only neighborhoods.[11]

The homeowners were so terrified that they frantically moved out in droves and sold their homes to the developers for pennies on the dollar. That form of trickery is called "blockbusting" and these greedy property developers were just getting started. After initiating white flight and buying the houses at lowball prices the same businessmen turned around and dramatically hiked up the price of the homes and sold them to desperate Black buyers. The aspiring Black homeowners couldn't get FHA insurance so they signed contracts that stated if they missed a single payment on the 30-year loan the home and all equity reverted back to the seller. After a few decades the developers made billions of dollars from buying the homes for cheap and then selling at a great premium only to eventually confiscate them. The Baltimore victim's subsequent lawsuit was unsuccessful.

Decades of preventing Blacks from profiting from real estate has had a profound impact. While most Blacks were denied loans to buy or repair homes the majority of middle-class white families gained their wealth from home equity. Today Black American income on average is about 60% of average white incomes and Black America controls less than 5% of the wealth while white America controls 90%. The huge difference between a 60% income ratio and a 5% wealth ratio is almost entirely attributable to racist federal housing policies implemented through the 20th century.[12] Black America missed out on billions in home equity and was denied generational wealth due to the FHA's discriminatory lending restrictions from 1934 until 1968, the year the Fair Housing Act was passed. While most of these policies have been abolished the impact has never been remedied and their consequences persist.

Nothing in this world is better at suppressing racial liberation and immortalizing oppression than white supremacy. With 500 years of practice the backers of white supremacy rely on a proven formula to reinforce roadblocks to racial parity. When Black progress finally defies insurmountable racist barriers the Caucasian strategy is to customarily reject defeat by deploying a secondary assault in order to facilitate perpetuating ongoing oppression and abuse. The forces of white supremacy create infinite obstruction by subsidizing continual resistance through an array of obstacles used to achieve or support the initial goal.

For example, first it was slavery and after that was defeated sharecropping and convict labor leasing became the backup plans for misappropriating Black labor. To control Black birthrate the first weapon used was The Negro Project, better known as abortions. That was not effective enough so mass incarceration was added to the cause, and when abortions and incarceration was not adequate, same-sex and youth castration was strongly encouraged, even incentivized. When it came time to use chemical warfare against the Black community at first it was hard alcohol, then heroin, then crack-cocaine followed by cheap malt liquor. When deplorable cops harm the community the police chief protects them. If the chief fires them the union fends for them. If they still get terminated they can rely on arbitrators to safeguard their employment.

When Black organizations were a threat the first method of containment was to smear the organization. That was followed by using eminent domain to prevent their operation from renting office space. When that was insufficient it was time to bring in the FBI and disrupt and destroy through wiretaps, misinformation, prison and assassinations. When that didn't suffice the next phase was cooptation in order to finance Black organizations, substituting confrontational sit-ins and rebellious street protests with limited judicial challenges. To completely control "black" organizations they replaced popular grass roots figures chosen by Blacks with either rappers or appointed unknown and worthless management to help steered them away from self-sufficiency. When it came time to neutralize Black leadership altogether the first weapons of choice were intimidation, then prison, then exile and then the final solution, assassinations. When killing and hard power was no longer practical they stopped murdering and started co-opting Black leaders through cushy corporate jobs and powerless positions inside political parties and organizations funded by them. The first thing Africans had to defeat was white Arab slavery, then white European slavery, then they had to conquer colonization and currently they are fighting neocolonialism.

Likewise, the first effort to fight fair housing was brutality and cross burnings and signage, followed by using white-only covenants and abusing eminent domain laws, eventually complimenting that with unfair predatory lending practices. Today those weapons and tactics are ineffective so sabotaging real estate wealth has culminated into systems known as "urban renewal" and gentrification. Frequently the sections where Black communities were historically forced to settle happened to be situated on prime real estate. Numerous predominately Black areas are near downtown, the airport, shopping, beaches or the central business district. Decades of poverty and segregation designated these areas as official Black zones until a white-powered cabal consisting of the U.S. Government, real estate businesses and developers realize that powerless people are living on a geographical gold mine. The scheme calls for the white establishment to buy out Black homeowners and businesses for peanuts and then revitalize the area. Upon completion of this new upscale development the original residents can't afford to live there so others move in and set up businesses and just like that, Blacks have been displaced by non-Blacks. This is called gentrification and it habitually happens to Black and Latinos across the United States.

In other instances building roads and freeways are used to fracture and destroy Black and Latino communities. The FHA's *Underwriting Manual* also recommended that highways be used to separate Blacks from white neighborhoods. Former US Secretary of Transportation

Anthony Foxx grew up in a neighborhood that was devastated by a freeway and he spoke on how the freeway systems contribute to poverty and inequality. According to Foxx "in the first 20 years of the federal interstate system alone, highway construction displaced over one million US citizens, most of them Black." Established Black working class or strong middle class and even affluent areas are all targets for white hindrance to gaining real estate wealth.[13]

Hayti, Durham North Carolina is a prime example of using roads to ruin select communities. In the 1880s Blacks moved to Hayti to work in the tobacco warehouses. The founders of this independent economic zone named the area after Haiti—a successful slave revolt anointed Haiti the first free independent Black republic in the Western hemisphere. Two of Hayti's founders, John Merrick and James Shepard also founded North Carolina Mutual Life Insurance Company which became the richest Black owned company during that time, and the company has over 200 million dollars in assets today.

Merrick and Shepard also created a land development company that built many of the homes and businesses in Hayti. By 1907 and two generations removed from slavery, Hayti became the first Black community to become fully self-sufficient boasting hotels, theaters, libraries, grocery markets and clothing stores. In 1910 they built The Lincoln Hospital, staffed by Black doctors and nurses as well as North Carolina University. At its peak Hayti had over 200 Black owned businesses. In 1910 and 1911 iconic figures W.E.B. Du Bois and Booker T. Washington visited Hayti respectfully. Here is how Du Bois described Hayti:

> "Today, there is a singular group in Durham where a black man may get up in the morning from a mattress made by a black man, in a house which a black man built out of lumber which black men cut and planed; he may put on a suit which he bought at a colored haberdashery and socks knit at a colored mill; he may cook victuals from a colored grocery on a stove which black men fashioned; he

> may earn his living working for colored men, be sick in a colored hospital and buried from a colored church; and the Negro insurance society will pay his widow enough to keep his children in school. This is surely progress."[14]

By practicing group economics Hayti citizens and the business class achieved self-sufficiency but racism locked them out of the political system. In 1958 an all-white planning commission targeted them with a large freeway project which ultimately fragmented Hayti. Less than 10 years later the total obliteration of this once incredibly successful Black homeland was complete. The before and after images of Hayti couldn't be more stark and anyone looking at Hayti today would never know that it once stood for Black excellence.

Another example of urban renewal destroying a successful Black economic zone is Jackson Ward in Richmond, Virginia. In the early 1900s so many Black businesses transpired that the area is widely regarded as the "birthplace of Black capitalism." In fact the area had so many banks, insurance companies and investment groups that it was the original Black Wall Street. In 1903 Maggie Walker became the first woman of any color to found and become president of an American bank. Jackson Ward was not only a Black economic hub but also renowned for its vibrant nightlife with celebrities like Joe Louis, Duke Ellington, Billie Holiday, Lena Horne, Cab Calloway and many others frequenting local night spots.[15]

Jackson Ward's decline was a result of an all-white city council implementing a plan to "revitalize" Jackson Ward. In the 1950s the dismantling was assured after an all-white Virginia State Assembly voted to run Interstate 95 through Jackson Ward. People displaced move to other cities which caused overcrowding while relocation lowered Jackson Ward's tax base. Most victims of urban improvement programs never fully recover from what can be accurately described as community eradication programs. These freeway systems result in disconnected communities and torn down buildings which creates dead zones where successful commerce once thrived.

Clearly these white planning commissions have ulterior motives for consistently labeling affluent Black communities as "blight" and then using freeway systems and revitalization plans to selectively dispose of so called blight. The freeways also serve to provide a concrete segregation barrier to keep "undesirables" confined to a designated area. Instead of living on the wrong side of the tracks many Blacks and Latinos live on the wrong side of the freeway. There are literally dozens of these examples all across the United States.

The world would be bearing witness to a proliferation of impressive independent economic centers contributing billions of dollars to Black wealth, image and the global economy if managers of white supremacy didn't sabotage progress with laws, police, vigilantes and renewal schemes. Supporters of white supremacy dependably exclude how a final circumstance materialized and instead enjoy focusing solely on the end results of their seditious actions. For instance, the far-right leaves out the role white supremacy played in causing inadequacies and instead illustrate Black deficiencies as a means to epitomize genetic inferiority. Their foundation is based on underscoring Black destitution while omitting their role in creating the poverty, only to rhetorically ask "can you imagine if Black people were running the world? Just imagine a world without us whites." They maintained jim crow for100 years, denied Black America government loans for decades and if Blacks still somehow prospered they install highways through successful Black areas. Those facts are ignored and replaced with the conclusion of their handy-work, "Black neighborhoods are terrible."

Places like Hayti, Jackson Ward and Greenwood Oklahoma are the embodiment of Black determination and exemplify greatness against all odds while concurrently demonstrating the extent oppressors will go to stop it. The efforts of determined Black activists combined with supportive white people could lead to reparations. In North Carolina, the city of Asheville "apologizes and makes amends for its participation in and sanctioning of the enslavement of Black people," "for its enforcement of segregation and its accompanying discriminatory practices" and "for carrying out an urban renewal program that destroyed multiple, successful Black communities."[16]

What: Character Assassination and Negative Media Depictions

When: From Day One

How: By Any Means Necessary

Why: To Give White Society and the World a Built-In Reason to Hate Blacks, Rendering Them as Non-Competitive and Laying the Foundation to Justify Genocide

Who: White Controlled Media, Especially Hollywood

Category: Teaching Black People Self-Hatred, Fostering Global Hatred

Status: In Full Effect

Brokers of white supremacy have invested in messaging the world that the color Black is cursed or that bad things happen to Black people because they deserved it. One way they do so is by creating negative programming like *Jerry Springer, Maury Povich, The First 48, LockUp, Lockdown, LAPD Live, Cops, Gangland* and of course the evening news. Let's take a hypothetical look at a typical day for many viewers. If a person woke up and immediately turned on the morning news they will likely be exposed to some street crime associated with someone black. Upon hearing the "black sounding name" viewers conclude it comes as no surprise. With the morning still young there is nothing better to do than to watch some *Jerry Springer*. With more black pathology on display for the better part of an hour the takeaway can only be that black people are at best weirdoes and ghetto jackasses and at worst suitable for removal. Since this typical day has just gotten started with black pathology as the centerpiece many viewers switch over to *The Maury Povich Show* after the Springer show. This is where viewers will conclude that blacks are some of the most financially irresponsible and promiscuous people on Earth…maybe eradication isn't so bad idea after all.[17]

By midday viewers have been taught that blacks are criminals, ghetto trash and reckless idiots and the viewers are not even done letting the television teach them about black people. After Maury goes off this hypothetical viewer decides to run some errands. But dinner time provides an opportunity to acquire an advanced televised education regarding black people. For many people, watching the evening news during dinner time is a long-held tradition and this viewer is no exception. For the next hour, over dinner and during digestion the viewer will be sporadically shown images of black people accused of crime. Even when the crime rate noticeably drops the evening news never reflects that decrease because profiting from the miseducation of society takes priority.

The routine subliminal messages of poverty and violence will be intertwined with "inner city" coverage all the way to the weather and sports segments. The viewer is now full on both their dinner and television coverage of Black America but the evening is still young so they check the TV guide hoping to defeat boredom. What do you know; the TV guide says there is a 12-hour marathon of the crime reality show, *The First 48*. With half the marathon already over the viewer tunes in to catch the rest of it. After six hours of being bombarded with images of black men killing and snitching the viewer considers turning in for the night. But during the airing of each episode of *The First 48* there were constant advertisements for another reality cop show called *LAPD Live.* After watching a few episodes of *LAPD Live* the viewer finally calls it a night.[18]

Reminiscing the pathological programming while tossing and turning with recollections of an impending bloated cable bill, and with more addictive pathology cloaked as entertainment available 24-hours; the viewer forgoes sleeping and chooses to continue consuming malignant *programming*—television transmission that often displays unlucky inferior Blacks and highly regarded white society. Unable to sleep the viewer decides the best way to "naturally" slumber is by watching a few hours of the late night prison documentary *LockUp,* a reasonable and most befitting way to blissfully doze off and end the day.

That fictional summary describes typical American television viewing habits and is a reality for millions of people. American television doesn't give many options as the morning programming consists of neurotic court shows, trash programming like Jerry Springer, soap operas and of course the news, most often featuring blacks. Throughout the day there are various talk shows and more news showcasing high-speed chases or gun violence, oftentimes involving blacks. In the evening there is more news followed by television's primetime programming, which is rarely favorable to Blacks. The end result is the vast majority of people who watch such programming inevitably see them mostly as buffoons, ghetto, violent criminals, losers and convicts.

Even a casual look at the white resume reveals fixation and an incredible effort to showcase Blacks as worthy of every ounce of resentment a person can muster. Apparently since many white people fear and hate Blacks the entire world should too. In the U.S. white controlled mainstream media uses its power to depict Blacks in the light that they want them to be seen by the rest of the world. The popularity of "black face" alone says that white power has historically been interested in shaping how others view Black people. White media distributes their desired black image to the world via talk shows, music, movies, the evening news and a variety of other television "programming." The end result is profound and has worldwide ramifications. For example, many well-educated Blacks travel to Southeast Asia for teaching assignments only to be told face-to-face that because they are Black they won't be hired. Oftentimes these professionals end up struggling to secure low-level teaching jobs while unqualified and uneducated whites are preferred for top teaching assignments.

In the U.S. the Black image has been so warped that there is never any consensus regarding video-recorded, obviously unjust police shootings/killings because there is always justification for murdering unarmed Black people. Black victims of police brutality must be above reproach and without the slightest lifetime blemish in order to be seen as human beings. When an unarmed Black man is repeatedly shot the rationale ranges from his cell phone or key-ring looked like a gun to somehow black-on-black crime justifies it. For example, millions of people (including Uncle Toms) hoped there would be footage of George Floyd resisting arrest because such footage would have completely exonerated the ten minute lynching. When no such resistance was shown some people highlighted his irrelevant criminal record while others blamed his heart or drugs in his system. For many people **there is no such thing as an innocent or undeserving Black man/woman when it comes to police abuse.** The lousy image that media has created for Black people extends to Africa too. No amount of development in Africa seems to change the advertised impression that all Africans hopelessly live in mud-huts and suffer from AIDS and famine.

On the other hand, Caucasian overseers have submitted to the world a resume based on a well-developed and ongoing public relations campaign that presents them as clean, needed, smart, upwardly mobile and likeable. Juxtapose that with their total destruction of Black image resulting in the entire world categorically detesting Black people. One bizarre end result is if you traveled to any country that went to war with a white governed nation, and conducted man-on-the-street-interviews inquiring about racial preferences it would almost unanimously favor white society.

If you traveled to Japan, China, Mexico or Vietnam and pointed out that Blacks have never militarily harmed them followed by itemizing factual white warmongering history including murder, rape, atom bombs, rewriting history, colonization, stolen land and ransacking artifacts the choice for whites would be swift and near unanimous. If you also reminded them that the racial slurs that were created for their specific group was developed by members in white society they wouldn't budge in their decision to prefer whites over Blacks. By controlling Black image the adherents of white supremacy and nationalism can assure that the rest of the world hates Black people as much as they do. Many Blacks all over the world have been so extremely impacted by the portrayal of both Black people and white society, that skin-bleaching is a chronic problem anywhere there are Black people.

The total sacking of Black image begs to ask one question, why? North Koreans, Chinese, Russians and Iranians don't experience this, and they come from countries that are or have been hostile towards the U.S. Why is controlling and abasing Black image so critical to white supremacy strategists? The end results of destroying Black image have numerous advantages including relegating Black people to noncompetitive status in many spheres. Illuminating Blacks negatively has another benefit; by the time white media finishes slandering Black image the average viewer won't have time to really look at or scrutinize white society and their inhumane history. By using negative rap music, drugs, AIDS and alternative lifestyles, prison and poverty Black people are a hated laughing stock of the world.

Vandalizing Black image also serves the purpose of selling the world on a few narratives such as "slavery was good for Blacks, just look at their neighborhoods and the condition of Africa," and "Blacks can't manage any city or country, just look at the big cities in America and Africa," always omitting any role white supremacy played. Another tremendous benefit is that white youth is automatically scripted to look down on Blacks and are inoculated against viewpoints that indict the white establishment. From growing up with the built-in teachings that Blacks are inferior and violent, by adulthood people have been systematically taught many racist talking points infused with the fundamental tenets of white supremacy—conveyed by the controllers of white supremacy themselves. Media keeps racism alive to make it easy to teach white youth and society in general to hate Blacks. White Westerners refuse to credit Africans for developing modern civilization and the result is collective rejection of Black authority, innovations, leadership and human rights. Most people base their opinions strictly on what they view on television so controlling what people see is tantamount to controlling how they feel and what they believe.

White media and academia could highlight Black contributions to the world by explaining known facts and history to help foster respect for Blacks. Instead educators misinform the youth and withhold revealing that the same reviled Black race started out as the progenitors of modern civilization and also played a critical role in developing western civilization. Consequently many people go to their graves never knowing that a Black woman was instrumental in developing GPS systems (Dr. Gladys West), or that a Black slave taught America how to inoculate against disease (Onesimus), or that the richest man to ever walk the Earth was a Black African, (Mansa Musa), or that a Black man invented the television remote control (Joseph N. Jackson). It comes as a complete shock that a Black man patented the helicopter (Paul E. Williams) or that the first company to create automobiles was Black-owned (CR Patterson) or that Jack Simmons Jr. was a successful oil baron for several decades. Under white rule society is rarely taught that Blacks invented the air conditioner, fire escape and the whiskey Jack Daniels. Since these facts are denied, stolen or hidden away, when people eventually discover this information it causes kneejerk denials leading to immediate shock followed by the predictable question "well, what happened?"

The honest answer to the question "what happened" would expose the real resume of white society—currently cloaked away from view to hide the widespread and incomputable crimes committed against humanity. Another benefit to sabotaging Black image is that when it comes time to implement a more aggressive form of genocide the world will have already been conditioned to hate Blacks and conclude "good riddance." Images of blacks as violent and ignorant and associated with AIDS and crack, genetically inferior, complete with effeminate men and masculine women (Hitler rounded up homosexuals) sends the message that the world is better off without them.

After observing the contemporary status of Blacks anyone who hears about the former greatness of the Black man and woman has a right to ask "what happened?" Space constraints prohibit offering a detailed explanation to anyone honestly asking. But when far-right proponents ask "If Africa and Blacks were so great, than what happened," the answer should be quite succinct. A two-step process is the best way for a white racist to understand how Blacks transformed from greatness to currently underdeveloped. Step one is for them to quickly locate the nearest mirror, and the second step requires them to count to three and then look right into it. There is where they will find the answer to their infamous and usually sarcastic question.

What: Controlling Networks like Black Entertainment Television (BET)

What: Mind Control

When: Year 2000

How: By Purchasing the Network

Why: To Control and Influence Every Aspect of Black Life

Who: Viacom, White Power

Category: Mind Control

Status: In Effect

At best Black Entertainment Television (BET) is a wolf in sheep's clothing offering at the most mediocre broadcasting while eschewing fundamental redeeming value. Fully controlling another group is certainly not limited to controlling their finances, life expectancy and fertility rate but also includes their musical taste, politics, diet, opinions, trends, fashions and news. This fact is not lost on the attendants of white supremacy as they profit off of keeping Black people beleaguered while simultaneously influencing every aspect of their lives. Reaching an estimated 90 million people with a slogan "Streaming Black Culture," the white-owned network has always been under fire for its negative programming featuring dreadful rap music, re-runs of recycled sitcoms, promiscuity and violence. Apparently it is asking too much to desire consistent educational documentaries, substantive Black movies, and positive messages of uplift or efforts to instill pride in Black America.

Wishing it could be said that the current programming is a drop off from the original programming, the initial programming wasn't much better as it focused on infomercials, garbage rap music and psychic hotlines. Under the original CEO and Black founder Bob Johnson,

BET appealed to the lowest common denominator and maintained bottom feeder status for the duration of Johnson's reign. As BET critic Holly Bass says, "BET doesn't even begin to scratch the surface when it comes to representing the diversity of our people and seems to make little effort to match the quality seen on other cable outlets." [19]

In 2020 the Fox News Corporation also got into the business of controlling Black image and messages and launched a streaming service called Fox Soul, complete with the slogan Celebrate Black Culture. But when the highly revered Black leader Louis Farrakhan was scheduled to appear on the network a few white people protested and he was promptly canceled, proving how unauthentic Black networks owned by white people truly are. Farrakhan was scheduled to appear and deliver a speech about racism over the 4th of July but was canceled due to objections by the Anti Defamation League and an unimportant CNN commentator named John Tapper. Fox has never caved in to liberal opposition as quickly as they did when a few extremist liberals protested broadcasting a speech by Farrakhan on a network aimed at Blacks, not white liberals or Jews.

Tapper did not complain about Don Lemon interviewing Farrakhan for CNN years earlier nor did Farrakhan say anything inflammatory. Tapper complained that Farrakhan was against "turning men into women and women into men" and he pointed out that Farrakhan said homosexuals were degenerates. What he failed to mention is that this lifestyle meets the very definition of degenerate. The dictionary says degenerate means "anything that lessens or degenerates" and same-sex behavior does exactly that by lowering birthrates and destroying civilizations. Heterosexuality generates and populates, homosexuality degenerates and depopulates. But any factual statement that shines a negative light on white Jews or the same-sex agenda is automatically condemned as homophobic and anti-Semitism and therefore prohibited under white rule. Tapper wouldn't complain if Fox Soul aired 8 hours of cross-dresser RuPaul dancing around in a g-string or if two 10-year-old girls were kissing or about gratuitous violence featuring drive-by shootings.

It should be abundantly clear why Blacks should never support any white-owned media aimed at Black viewers. If a Black-owned network arose and became highly successful it is guaranteed that white power would offer a large sum of money attempting to purchase the network. If successful the first thing they would do is ban select Black leaders and promote alternative lifestyles and pathology. Somehow white Jews, who comprise about 2% of the American population are above reproach alongside homosexuals. Since Farrakhan speaks facts about those two demographics he is not allowed any air time on this white-owned "Black network." The people who complained about Farrakhan don't even watch or support Fox Soul and yet Fox was more concerned about white non-viewers than their actual Black viewership who patronizes their commercial sponsors. A few people who don't even watch Fox Soul can tell Black viewers what they can and cannot see.

The cancellation happened during the height of the George Floyd protests and a time when the U.S. was being confronted over centuries of racism towards Blacks and yet a popular Black leader was still censored because a tiny white faction objected. No amount of Black support for the minister could reverse the decision to cancel the appearance of one of the greatest Black leaders in the history of America. Even if the minister guaranteed to avoid offending anyone he was not allowed free speech. Blacks should boycott any network aimed at Black viewers but owned by non-Blacks, period. John Tapper and white Jews have once again reminded Blacks they are living behind enemy lines and must establish their own media and avoid anything owned by the ushers of white supremacy. At no time do whites operate any Black network, record label or organization the same way Blacks would and for that very reason white power covets owning Black media outlets and controlling the messaging.

What: Controlling Rap Music

When: 1980s to Present

How: By Investing Billions of Dollars into Controlling the Genre, Converting Rap into a Killing Machine, Then Steering it Away From Anthems That Would Highlight Racism or Unify Blacks

Why: To Promote Destructive Behavior, Fill-Up Prisons and Graveyards While Creating an Image of Blacks That is Easily Hated, Thus Laying the Foundation for Aggressive Genocide Campaigns

Who: A Cartel Consisting of White Investors and Managers, Politicians, Sell-Out Black Troublemakers along with Corporate American Companies involved in Brewing and Distilling Alcohol

Category: Population Control, Operation Prison Pipeline

Status: Exemption, Untouchable

At some point one must ponder, "Can white people be any more wickedly ingenious in attacking Black people?" It starts to feel like members of the assailant race never miss an opportunity to control or destroy the Black populous. Only in the U.S. does a dominant culture offer colossal wealth to the criminal class of a despised group just to strengthen universal hatred and negatively influence their youth. Criminalizing rap music is a good way to reinforce racial animosity and mislead many impressionable and fatherless Black youth into practicing criminal behavior resulting in prison and early death. White people offer rappers vast treasures that would make the average man sell out his own mother, let alone his racial demographic. Violent rap music leads Black youth to behave irresponsibly and sponsoring it is another way the custodians of white power ensure many Blacks enters privately-owned prison-industrial complexes across the U.S. This isn't a hollow view as there are persistent reports and evidence of a concerted effort to use rap music to overfill U.S. prisons and apparently, it worked. According to a person with firsthand knowledge, music company executives invested in the prison industrial complex and then conspired to glorify criminal activity through rap music to help pack the prisons.

An article written by someone claiming to be present during a meeting that proposed using rap music to promote a lifestyle conducive to prison and death can be found online. Here are parts of a written confession from an anonymous insider who allegedly witnessed the entire proposal.

> After more than 20 years, I've finally decided to tell the world what I witnessed in 1991, which I believe was one of the biggest turning point in popular music, and ultimately American society. I have struggled for a long time weighing the pros and cons of making this story public as I was reluctant to implicate the individuals who were present that day. So I've simply decided to leave out names and all the details that may risk my personal well being and that of those who were, like me, dragged into something they weren't ready for.
>
> Between the late 80's and early 90's, I was what you may call a "decision maker" with one of the more established company in the music industry. I came from Europe in the early 80's and quickly established myself in the business. The industry was different back then. Since technology and media weren't accessible to people like they are today, the industry had more control over the public and had the means to influence them anyway it wanted. This may explain why in early 1991, I was invited to attend a closed door meeting with a small group of music business insiders to discuss rap music's new direction. Little did I know that we would be asked to participate in one

> of the most unethical and destructive business practice I've ever seen.

He continues:

> Our casual chatter was interrupted when we were asked to sign a confidentiality agreement preventing us from publicly discussing the information presented during the meeting. Needless to say, this intrigued and in some cases disturbed many of us. The agreement was only a page long but very clear on the matter and consequences which stated that violating the terms would result in job termination. We asked several people what this meeting was about and the reason for such secrecy but couldn't find anyone who had answers for us. A few people refused to sign and walked out. No one stopped them. I was tempted to follow but curiosity got the best of me. A man who was part of the "unfamiliar" group collected the agreements from us.
>
> The subject quickly changed as the speaker went on to tell us that the respective companies we represented had invested in a very profitable industry which could become even more rewarding with our active involvement. He explained that the companies we work for had invested millions into the building of privately owned prisons and that our positions of influence in the music industry would actually impact the profitability of these investments. I remember many of us in the group immediately looking at each other in confusion. At the time, I didn't know what a private prison was but I wasn't the only one. Sure enough, someone asked what these prisons were and what any of this had to do with us. We were told that these prisons were built by privately owned companies who received funding from the government based on the number of inmates.

The author of the letter claimed that after he and three other people heard the idea they became so irate that the meeting turned chaotic and they were forcibly removed from the meeting at gunpoint. He also said it was reiterated that the decision was much bigger than the music industry and no amount of protesting would matter. Out of the lengthy letter this paragraph was the most telling:

> As the months passed, rap music had definitely changed direction. I was never a fan of it but even I could tell the difference. Rap acts that talked about politics or harmless fun were quickly fading away as gangster rap started dominating the airwaves. Only a few months had passed since the meeting but I suspect that the ideas presented that day had been successfully implemented. It was as if the order has been given to all major label executives. The music was climbing the charts and most companies were more than happy to capitalize on it. Each one was churning out their very own gangster rap acts on an assembly line. Everyone bought into it, consumers included. Violence and drug use became a central theme in most rap music. I spoke to a few of my peers in the industry to get their opinions on the new trend but was told repeatedly that it was all about supply and demand. Sadly many of them even expressed that the music reinforced their prejudice of minorities.[20]

The informant quit the music business in 1993 and since then the controllers of foul rap music have made a hefty profit from their investments. Rappers continue to provide incendiary music that assures a steady flow of inmates, including many rap artists themselves. What truly supports the allegations in the confession letter is how executives continue to churn out active gang-bangers who sign multi-million dollar contracts while actively committing the same crimes they rap about, only to eventually be killed or incarcerated. White music executives are not allowing their own sons and daughters the opportunity to make millions of dollars as a gangster rapper. The white supremacists who are managing rap music are out of control and demonstrate their impunity through the horrific rap lyrics commonly passed off as entertainment. Evidently suit-wearing white extremists control rap because this powerful musical medium rarely discusses anything that is in the best interest of the Black community. Their Black Judases are co-conspirators who justify the poisonous psycho-babble by relying on that tired line "I'm just rapping about what I see."

They see hundreds of thousands of people going to work and school every day but only rap about the 10-100 gang members in the neighborhood. A few things serve as complete giveaways that rap music is systematically used to funnel Blacks into prisons. For young Black males the music has been an established part of the prison feeder system for over 30 years yet during discussions of prison reform violent rap music is never mentioned for consideration to address. Atrocious rap music is untouchable and has exempt status like many other weapons used against Blacks. Another indication of white supremacist control is how violent street rap suddenly incorporated alternative lifestyles into the performers and songs. With a targeted audience of persuadable Black youth and no demand for "gay rap", the executive directors of white supremacy monetized yet another genocidal feeder system to further guarantee minimizing Black fertility rates.

The secret meeting obvious happened based on the contrast of rap today compared to its beginnings, and how Black society would operate rap if they were in charge of it. If the real Black community had their way rap music would either be eliminated or only cover topics like love, police brutality, racism, unity and advancement. Obviously the current anthems focuses on everything opposite of a Black agenda such as killing, getting high and drunk, selling drugs, debasing your fellow Black man and woman, prison and death. Does that sound like real Blacks or even decent whites are managing rap music? In discussing gangster rap, on page 237 *The American Directory of Certified Uncle Toms* put it this way,

> If the larger Black community had had a say in the matter, NWA would have remained marginalized—an insignificant gaggle of riff-raff nuisance in need of reeducation; but Vibe reports that a white Jewish promoter name Jerry Heller began managing and aggressively

> promoting NWA to white record companies, one of which signed the group to a major recording contract.[21]

It cannot possibly be more clear that white supremacists are running rap because the white controllers experience people they know personally going to prison and being shot and killed, and yet won't stop producing the despicable music that is destroying their "friends" or the Black race.

Thanks to white financiers some blacks deliberately lead impressionable people into a life of crime through a hip-hop culture riddled with messages of thug life, promiscuity, prison and fratricide. Young black males can be open gang members or out on bail after committing a murderous drive-by shooting, only to get a million dollar contract to perform violent music that promotes pathology and glorifies crime and prison.

This is criminal and the American politicians stand indicted for allowing such treacherous music to exist and in fact if the rap anthems suddenly included harming white Jews, animals and the same-sex community, the genre would suddenly and unequivocally end. When Rick Ross did a *single lyric* about date rape in a song that otherwise glorified killing Blacks he was arbitrarily fired for having the audacity. Many rappers don't realize it but not only are they sell-outs but to some they easily eclipse the traditional Uncle Tom in harming Black people.[22]

A rapper known as Willie D offers interesting commentary regarding daily topics and one day actress Stacy Dash was in the news. Willie D made his disdain for Stacy clear because she is a black supporter of the far-right. He really lamented Stacy but the question is does he have any room to talk? Sure, Dash has gone on record with anti-Black rhetoric that one expects to hear from pundits like Sean Hannity or Rush Limbaugh or on Fox News. But Willie D was a part of a rap group (Geto Boys) that was notorious for music that promoted gang life and pathology which motivated some listeners to engage in violence against other Black people. In fact one member of the group quit because of the high number of young black men harming other Blacks, inspired by their music. Selling Black people out isn't limited to those who traditionally do so but includes rappers who use lyrics that derail Black progress and destroy Black lives.[23]

Omitting the billions of dollars collected annually, here is a list of benefits that white people get from promoting violent rap music.

- Profit from filling up prisons by promoting criminal behavior.
- By filling up prisons rap music lowers fertility rates—genocide.
- Promotes pathologies like foul language, drugs, violence, dangerous alternative lifestyles, and alcohol usage which shortens lifespan and is another contributing factor for Black extermination.
- Promotes multi-hatred; i.e. self-hatred and general hatred from other demographics through reinforcing stereotypes while popularizing characteristics that are easy to hate, such as scraggly bum attire, ghetto vernacular and behavior, educational failure, promiscuity, irresponsibility and gang violence. The self-hatred can also lead to suicide, nihilism and black homicide, another form of genocide.
- Helps lay the foundation for more aggressive forms of genocide as Blacks are seen as useless criminals worthy of removal.
- Most rap is a continuation of the minstrel shows historically used to destroy Black image. "Rap" has replaced "minstrels" to teach the world that Blacks are violent, foolish and drug dealers. Thanks to rap the slogan "I'm a real Black man" changed to *"I'm a real nigga"* overnight.
- Rap music divides Black America. Many Blacks remember the days when they often called each other "brother" or "sister" instead of "bitch" and of course the favorite disparaging word, "nigga." That ignorant word is ubiquitous and used for

everyone and everything, including a white man in a suit, a beauty contestant, police officers, a successful Black businessman, a valedictorian, a housewife, a second grader, dogs, birds or a wobbly table leg. Adherents of white supremacy never miss a way to introduce topics or weapons that will cause a civil war—they are permanently dedicated to dividing and conquering Black people. Whites have always counted on Uncle Toms to help control, divide and influence the masses and many rap performers are being used exactly for that purpose. The most treasonous Uncle Tom is the fratricidal gang-banger who harms other Blacks over trivial reasons such as colors or a facial expression.

- Rap music makes it nearly impossible to reclaim stolen Black history because by the time people get a load of the English-butchering, uneducated, gun-toting emotional clown influenced by rap they find it impossible to believe that modern math, medicine or any greatness came from such a lost, idiotic low-life representative of the human race. Creating a caricature of Blacks in film and music allows easy discreditation.
- Controlling rap music allows the wardens of white supremacy to control trends and trends are as powerful as religion. Some negative trends supported by rap include sagging pants, scowl face expressions, violently settling disputes, disrespecting a hard work ethic, punctuating every sentence with "nigga" or "know what I'm sayin" and putting jewelry on your teeth.
- Some rap music promotes absolute ignorance not only reflected in speech impediments and dress but also educational outlook: "school and learning is for white people" is a motto for some rap artists and followers.
- Based on the influence of a certain type of rap music, possibly the biggest weapon the purveyors of white supremacy get from

rap is the power of "niggerization." A common view of whites and others is, "there are good Blacks, and then there are the niggers." Educated, well-spoken, polite Blacks wearing decent attire are still considered an N-Word but are much less likely to be treated like or called that. The ambassadors of white power are using rap music to breed and increase the kind of contemptible black people outfitted with "nigger" characteristics and easily despised, also laying the foundation for extermination.

- Music executives and politicians use rappers to replace grassroots political leadership with unread, uneducated misguided people who don't effectively represent Black interests. The white establishment wants Black leadership to be anything but the same as yesteryear and have little in common with well-spoken leaders like Malcolm X and Dr. King. Since white people have their way the chosen and legitimized Black "leadership" now consists of vulgar, jewelry wearing street thugs, former prostitutes, drug dealers and drive-by shooters often incapable of formulating a sentence without mangling the English language. They are encouraged to accompany other white-selected impotent Black leaders who support gay rights and benign neglect. What's next, politicians meeting with Black porn stars and treating them like "leaders?"[a]

---

[a] Ice Cube is Focused on The Black Agenda in Election, Says Biden and Trump Reached Out To Him! September 10, 2020, WorldStar Hip Hop, https://www.worldstarhiphop.com/videos/video.php?v=wshh7j0fjF 5zF7xoDiHE Ice Cube wisely rejected benign neglect. Regrettably, Biden sat down with lewd rapper, former sex-worker and self-admitted criminal who drugged and robbed men, "Cardi B," treating her like an insightful "leader." Also, days after scumbag "Lil Wayne" called women bitches, declared himself

Finally, rap lessened the shine for Blacks universally. So determined to ruin Black image, the caretakers of white power replaced R&B with rap music, but it will never be as fondly regarded as the beautiful music made by bygone R&B artists. That music is over 40-years-old with many songs revered and still played all over the world today. Artists like Marvin Gaye or Sade moved people to eternally love "soul" music and appreciate Black talents and culture. On the other hand many rap performers stay in and out of prison and help produce the kind of black people you hate to see coming.

This includes but is not limited to emotional and immature blacks who have meltdowns over the service in a fast-food restaurant and end up pushing the cash register onto the floor, climbing onto the counter and then repeatedly chanting in ghetto vernacular "You got me f----d up!" One hundred percent of them, one hundred percent of the drive-by shooters, one hundred percent of the black high school drop-outs, one hundred percent of blacks aged 18-40 in prison, one hundred percent of the gang-bangers love so-called gangster rap. In typical white fashion the mainstream media never reminds the Black-hating public that white entities make the most money from rap music and are largely responsible for the genre leading to crime and prison. Instead white power focuses on the end results of their handy work and blame Black skin and genetics for the horrendous outcomes. It is going to take

---

a "nigga" and pledged an allegiance to a street gang, President Trump met with him to discuss a financial agenda called The Platinum Plan. Why didn't Trump or Biden meet with professional economists? Why avoid intelligent and dedicated people like Dr. Umar Johnson, Dr. Boyce Watkins or Dr. Claud Anderson? See Lil Wayne promoting gang banging, I'm A Gang Banger. My Life Matters. Especially To My Bxxches, That Time Lil Wayne Said He's Not Down With BLM... Endorsing Trump Now!, October 29, 2020 WorldStar Hip Hop, https://worldstarhiphop.com/videos/video.php?v=wshh3XgEoEVu60VPZYwY

decades to undo the damage done by negative rap music, and the clock can't start ticking until it has ran its course.[24]

What: Mass Incarceration

When: 1980 to Present

How: Preventive Inaction, Advocating Criminal Activity through Entertainment, Bias Policing and Using "The War on Drugs" to fill Prisons Nationwide

Why: To Lower Birthrate and Secure Free Labor

Who: Politicians, Local, State and Federal Government, Law Enforcement, Hollywood, Crime-Promoting Rappers and the Whites who Control Rap Music

Category: Genocide, Slavery Extension

Status: Active, Defcon 1

The NAACP provides the following information regarding incarceration on their justice fact sheet:

Incarceration Trends in America

- Between 1980 and 2015 the number of people incarcerated in America increased from roughly 500,000 to over 2.2 million
- Today the United States makes up about 5% of the world's population and has 21% of the world's prisoners
- 1 in every 37 adults in the United States or 2.7% of the adult population is under some form of correctional supervision

Racial Disparities in Incarceration

- In 2014, Black Americans constituted 2.3 million or 34% of the total 6.8 million correctional population, by 2020 the percentage rose to nearly 40%
- Blacks are incarcerated at more than 5 times the rate of whites
- The imprisonment rate for Black women is twice that of Caucasian women
- Nationwide, Black American children represent 32% of children who are arrested, 42% of children who are detained, and 52% of children whose cases are judicially waived to criminal court
- Though Black Americans and Latinos make up approximately 32% of the U.S. population, they comprise 56% of all incarcerated people in 2015
- If Blacks and Latinos were incarcerated at the same rates as whites prison and jail populations would decline by nearly 40%

Drug Sentencing Disparities

- In the 2015 National Survey on Drug Use and Health, about 17 million whites and 4 million African Americans reported having used an illicit drug within the last month.
- Black Americans and whites use drugs at similar rates, but the imprisonment rate of Blacks for drug charges is almost 6 times that of whites.
- Black Americans represent 12.5% of illicit drug users, but 29% of those arrested for drug offenses and 33% of those incarcerated in state facilities for drug offenses.

Effects of Incarceration

- A criminal record can reduce the likelihood of a callback or job offer by nearly 50 percent. The negative impact of a criminal record is twice as large for Black American applicants.

- Infectious diseases are highly concentrated in corrections facilities: 15% of jail inmates and 22% of prisoners – compared to 5% of the general population – reported ever having tuberculosis, Hepatitis B and C, HIV/AIDS, or other STDs.
- In 2012 alone, the United States spent nearly $81 billion on corrections.
- Spending on prisons and jails has increased at triple the rate of spending on Pre-K-12 public education in the last thirty years.

Not long ago U.S. citizens boasted "we are the freest country in the world." At the time it was debatable, but today that debate would be a lopsided one at best. Nowadays citizenry deals with an erosion of civil liberties, a heavily regulated nanny-state, a surveillance state and the highest incarceration rate in the world, indicating the United States and freedom are not synonymous.[25]

What: COINTELPRO

When: 1956 to Present

How: Through Secrecy and Government Enforcement

Why: To Prevent Black People from Achieving Equality through Organizations and Leadership

Who: Law Enforcement

Category: The Decimation of Black Organizations

Status: Legalized, Active

U.S. Government-sponsored control of Black dissidents is hundreds of years old. Long before COINTELPRO was created the FBI was directly involved in dissident control. In 1922 the FBI masterminded the demolition of Marcus Garvey's organization known as the Universal Negro Improvement Association (UNIA). With over two million members, the FBI used Uncle Toms to infiltrate the UNIA and put in place the elements needed to convict Garvey on mail fraud, promptly leading to his deportation and the collapse of the UNIA. While the FBI routinely undermined dissent from its inception, in 1956 that goal became official so the bureau established COINTELPRO to accomplish that objective.

This counterintelligence program (COINTELPRO for short) was involved in squashing any movement the far-right considered a threat. Organizations headed by American Indians, homosexuals, women, Mexican Americans, communists and others were attacked and dissolved. By far the Black Power and civil rights movements bore the brunt of these efforts. At the top of the FBI's agenda was to obliterate groups like the Nation of Islam, Black Panther Party and Dr. King's Southern Christian Leadership Conference. The majority of the leaders of Black organizations were assassinated, imprisoned or exiled. Malcolm X was the victim of factional disputes instigated by the FBI. Before he was assassinated Martin Luther King was targeted with an elaborate scheme to drive him crazy or cause him to commit suicide and replace his leadership role with black "conservative" Samuel Pierce.[26]

The laughable pretense for attacking these organizations was to stop terrorism and insurgent behavior. On page 66 of *War at Home*, Brian Glick, weighs in on this deceitful claim:

> Equally preposterous as a justification for domestic covert action is the official pretense that it helps to prevent violence and terrorism within the United States. Under COINTELPRO, the FBI condoned and supported the racist violence of the Ku Klux Klan, the secret Army Organization, and other right-wing vigilantes…the vast

majority of the targets of domestic covert action have only engaged in peaceful protest.

On page 68 Glick continues:

> Taking into account the political beatings, shootings, and vandalism by the FBI and police, their aid to right-wing vigilantes, their provocation and incitement of brutal assaults on activists, and their outright assassinations of movement leaders, these government agencies are far away the primary source of political violence in the United States.[27]

White owned "black organizations" like the NAACP and Urban League were allowed to continue to exist because they expanded to address white Jewish concerns or were not attempting to truly gain racial equality. The most prestigious award given by the NAACP is the Spingarn medal. The medal is named after a white Jew name J.E. Spingarn. No white Jewish organization would ever offer an award named after a Black person, even though the first Jews were Black.[28] In the U.S. the only nationally independent Black controlled organization existing without white sponsorship and control is The Nation of Islam.

What: Falsely Claiming White People Started Modern Civilization

When: Unknown

How: By Denying Concrete Facts with a Straight Face and Showing Images of Primitive Africans and Mud-Hut Dwellings

Why: To Fortify the Myth of White Supremacy, Designate the Black Race to Inferior Status and Disconnect Black People from Having a Can-Do Attitude, also used To Justify Slavery and Promote Discrimination

Who: White Academia, Media and Supremacists

Category: Psychic Warfare, Genocide Conditioning

Status: In Effect

Denying Black people made any meaningful contributions to mankind or started modern civilization was necessary to justify treating Blacks like chattel and relegating them to bottom rung status. The fact that modern civilization was started by Black people at a time when whites were primitive defies every tenet supporting white supremacy and therefore must be denied. Provable ancient Black African history is found globally and has been parceled out to all other demographics. To do this white power must place white people all over the world and start modern history at 5,000-8,000 years ago, instead of including factual history and innovations that are 10,000 to 150,000-years-old—ancient innovations that usually defaults to Black Africans. When Black historians cite the concrete proof to other people now sitting on actual African history many claim "Blacks are stealing everyone's history/religion again."

This "little white lie" over starting modern civilization is a common talking point of ignorant people and used to justify racism. The misrepresentation that white Europeans started modern civilization has several functions including concealing the embarrassing fact that while Black Africans were modern and dominating world affairs, their white European counterparts were either not evolved into existence or still primitive and living in the Caucasus mountain cave systems of Europe. The fictional claim of starting civilization is an excellent way to boost white group self-esteem while disconnecting Blacks from high-achieving and reaping the benefits that accommodate a can-do attitude. Taking credit for establishing modern civilization is a way to thwart Blacks from repeating such greatness.

A book titled *Stolen Legacy* exposed the scale of Greek theft and fully discredits Greek philosophy as nothing more than African philosophy. The author, George James might have paid with his life for releasing facts that strike a blow to the white lie that Greek scholars are responsible for the foundation of western civilization, a lie now resting upon the twin pillars of fraudulent Greek history and misplaced Greek philosophy. In describing his book James wrote:

> The aim of the book is to establish better race relations in the world by revealing a fundamental truth concerning the contribution of the African continent to civilization. It must be born in mind that the first lesson in the humanities is to make a people aware of their contributions to civilization. And the second lesson is to teach them about other civilizations. By this dissemination of the truth about the civilization of individual peoples, a better understanding among them and a proper appraisal of each other should follow...Consequently, the book is an attempt to show that the true authors of Greek philosophy were not the Greeks, but the people of North Africa commonly called the Egyptians. And the praise and honor falsely given to the Greeks for centuries belong to the people of North Africa and therefore to the African continent. Consequently, this theft of the African legacy by the Greeks led to the erroneous world opinion that the African continent has made no contribution to civilization and that its people are naturally backward.
>
> This is the misrepresentation that has become the bases of race prejudice which has affected all people of color. For centuries the world has been misled about the original source of the arts and sciences. For centuries, Socrates, Plato and Aristotle have been falsely idolized as models of intellectual greatness. And for centuries the African continent has been called the Dark Continent because Europe coveted the honor of transmitting to the world the arts and sciences.[29]

There is no shortage of so-called white scholars who insist the builders of the pyramids and originators of modern civilization were white. The topic became so heated that in 1974 a symposium called The Peopling of Ancient Egypt and the Deciphering of the Meroitic Script was held in Cairo Egypt to settle the matter. A team of professionals who insisted Black people built the pyramids and created modern civilization was pitted against a panel of opponents to debate the topic in front of 20 neutral Egyptologists. It was no match. Led by celebrated African historian Cheikh Anta Diop, his team claimed the ancient Egyptians were clearly Black and they provided charts, graphs, dates of conquests, images, statues, artifacts, anthropology and archaeological evidence, DNA analysis and countless books written by Greek and other historians admitting ancient Egyptians were dark brown and Black skin. The evidence overwhelmed their opponents and greatly impressed UNESCO, the organization who sponsored the symposium. Opponents who claimed the ancient Egyptians were white were annihilated which forced the neutral judges and UNESCO to record their final analysis, reading in part:

> "Although the preparatory working paper sent out by UNESCO gave particulars of what was desired, not all participants had prepared communications comparable with the painstakingly researched contributions of Professors Cheikh Anta Diop and Obenga. There was consequently a real lack of balance in the discussions."[30]

Professional white liars had no answers to valid questions like "If Greece was the first European nation to develop 3,000 years ago, how did they build pyramids 2,000 years before that?" "Why would white people travel thousands of miles by foot and boat, 5,000 years ago, to begin civilization in Africa when they didn't previously do that in Europe? [31] To immediately get to the bottom of who started modern civilization the only thing anyone has to do is attempt to record ancient innovations found in Europe that date over 5,000-years-old. Try a head-to-head comparison with the innovations found in Africa and Europe that are between 3,000 to 40,000-years-old to determine where modern civilization really started. The research will confirm Africans started modern civilization in Africa and elsewhere. Additional research will show that white homo sapiens are estimated to be between 5,000 to the recently extended 8,000-years-old.[32]

Out of all the fabrications used to buttress so-called white supremacy the falsehood that white people developed the first modern civilization is the most preposterous and easiest to disprove. Because of that the promoters of this talltale must be willing to say just about anything to support it while ignoring what should be irrefutable facts that prove otherwise. The hard truth is white people had absolutely nothing to do with originating modern civilization and rejecting that reality leads racist supporters down a endless fairytale abyss of merry-go-round lying requiring advocates to moronically make it up as they go.

The end result is that some white people absurdly claim that King Tut, Hannibal and Nefertiti were white and the builders of the pyramids were paleface people who traveled from Europe to Africa to start modern civilization. An example of how easy it is to prove otherwise is to simply view King Tut and his wife painted on his throne and the people on the walls of his tomb. But when presented with irrefutable evidence the lying whitewashers will simply offer a brand new reconstructed lie to protect the original one. Presenting the unimpeachable facts is the best way to establish the true origins of modern civilization.

Modern math was in Africa for several thousand years before the earliest math to exit Europe called The Roman Numeral System was created, around 800BC.[33] In fact Europeans still use the Roman Numeral System today. It was incapable of computing high enough and considered "inferior" and ultimately abandoned for the modern math that originated in Africa and mostly used today. The first European nation to become modern is Greece, which occurred a mere 3,000 years ago. Luckily, for thousands of years Africans were given full credit as the creators of modern religion and civilization so consequently a litany of authors and books recorded the facts. Count Volney, Gerald Massey, Gaston Maspero, Demon Stewart, Charles Seignobee, Professor Heerens, Eugene Georg and scores of other historical writers, historians and scientists admitted Black Africans started modern civilization all over the world. Count Volney stated, "A race of men now rejected for their Black skin and wooly hair founded the study of the laws of nature, those civil and religious systems which still govern the universe."[34]

The vast majority of the famous Greek scholars admittedly traveled to Africa and sat at the feet of Black African teachers while attending what is today considered the oldest universities in the world, Waset in Thebes and Ipet Isut, found in Karnak, Kemet, today called Egypt. These universities are over 4,000-years-old. This bears repeating; the oldest universities in the world pre-date Greece by thousands of years and are located in Africa, complete with a highly advanced educational learning system called The Kemetic Mystery System. In Africa there are large scale, masterful concrete engravings depicting African students learning mathematics, astronomy, sciences, technology, architecture, writing, astrology, medicine, geometry, geography, religion, magic and grammar. The Kemetic Mystery System took 40 years to complete with none of the ancient Greek scholars fully completing it.[35]

There is extensive information available on both The Kemetic Mystery System and the ancient learning centers and this shouldn't be up for debate. Some high schools and colleges in Greece still teach that Africa directly influenced them. Greece passed their knowledge onto the Romans who eventually lost it and Europe reverted back to primitive living known as The Dark Ages. The Black Moors invaded Europe in 711AD and ruled for 781 years. These African rulers lived in posh mansions built by them and introduced a variety of crops and innovations. At its height, Córdova, the heart of Moorish territory in Spain, was the most modern city in Europe. The streets were well-paved, with raised sidewalks for pedestrians. During the night, ten miles of streets were illuminated by lamps using lavender fragrance oil. This was hundreds of years before there was a paved street in Paris or a street lamp in London. Cordova had 900 public baths that used modern plumbing.[36]

These Africans reestablished modern civilization in Europe by building a university system as well as over 70 libraries, one containing over 600,000 manuscripts. In return for rehabilitating Europe they required the white Europeans to pay financial tribute and allowed freedom and existing religion to remain intact. Because of those good deeds and fairness today some Europeans pay considerable homage to the Black Moors with statutes and tributes that still stand to this day. While white nationalists steadfast deny this historical record the Europeans have books and city blocks decorated with statues honoring Black Moors.[37]

The ancient innovations that came from inside Africa are equally astounding and speak directly to who started modern civilization. Africans were the first to discover and use paper and therefore the first to write books. The oldest libraries in the world are in Africa. Africans were the first to do C-sections and even taught the procedure to Europeans.

According to the U.S. National Library of Medicine:

> In 1879, for example, one British traveler, R.W. Felkin, witnessed cesarean section performed by Ugandans. The healer used banana wine to semi-intoxicate the woman and to cleanse his hands and her abdomen prior to surgery. He used a midline incision and applied cautery to minimize hemorrhaging. He massaged the uterus to make it contract but did not suture it; the abdominal wound was pinned with iron needles and dressed with a paste prepared from roots. The patient recovered well.[38]

Felkin concluded that this technique was well-developed and had clearly been employed for a long time. This information is provided by white European doctors whose writings and confessions are recorded in various medical journals currently found all over the world. Africans were the first to use modern medicine and perform cataract surgery, all 5,000 years ago. There is a model airplane in Africa that is well over 2000-years-old. Senet is a 5,000-year-old board game from Africa and the oldest prosthetic in the world is 3,000-years-old and found in Africa. Bowling and beekeeping started in Africa. Thousands of years ago Africans were sailing the great seas and traveling the world in what is known as the Khufu ship.[39]

There is a 43,000-year-old gold mine in Swaziland called the Ngwenya Mine. The two oldest math calculators in the world are both found in Africa. The world's oldest calculators are the Ishango bone, dated to be over 20,000-years-old and the Lembombo bone is estimated to be 43,000-years-old. Africans were the first to use toothbrushes and toothpaste, wigs, cosmetics, door locks, toilets, air conditioning and sewer systems. The calendar in use today was created by Black Africans 5,000-years-ago.[40] So-called white supremacy didn't limit their grand theft to physical innovations but also stole and rewrote the major religions that originated in Africa.

The images of a white Jesus are only about 500-years-old and many depictions actually feature a man named Cesar Borgia. Cesar's father was Pope Alexander VI who was the Pope from 1492 to 1503 and he commissioned Michael Angelo to paint his son as Jesus Christ. Initially there was a huge rift in the church over his decision but the image remained and over time it was accepted as Jesus. Cesar Borgia was rumored to be lovers with Leonardo Da Vinci, another painter who painted extravagant paintings of a white Jesus, Mary, the last supper and white angels.

Why does that matter? No bible describes Jesus as being white. Because the oldest image of Jesus Christ is allegedly a 2000-year-old image of a Black Jesus and his apostles located inside the Coptic Museum in Cairo, Egypt—painted when Jesus was possibly still alive.[41]

There is also a concrete engraving in Africa that allegedly shows an African Jesus who, incidentally, was named "Yeshua" and is still called that in parts of Africa to this day. Revelation 1:14-15 describes Jesus as having hair of wool and bronze skin. Not only is Queen Sheba allegedly buried in Ethiopia but Ethiopia is home to the most sacred artifact on Earth, the Ark of the Covenant. Ethiopia knew about Christianity 200 years before the Romans and Ethiopia is mentioned in the bible 45 times.[42] There is a 700 year old bible in Ethiopia, and all images of Jesus inside that book show him to be clearly Black. Also, images of the original Buddha shows that he had dreadlocks and basic research on Buddha and Islam reveals African origination.

What are some of the greatest contributions of Black Africans? (1) They discovered fire, writing and science, created advanced mathematics, the calendar we use today and originated modern civilization. (2) They educated the ancient world through the Kemetic Mystery System taught inside sophisticated learning centers in Africa. (3) They also restored civilization in Europe and saved barbaric white Europeans from The Dark Ages and a primitive existence. Stealing the credit and denying those African contributions is the best way to conceal being lowdown enough to enslave their teachers, the true pioneers of modern civilization and their saviors from The Dark Ages, thereby hiding how truly diabolical white power is. This information is easy to prove and readers are highly encouraged to do their own research. The author is confident that in doing so the average person will be reduced to either denial or shaking their head in total disgust.

What: Sharecropping

When: 1866 to 1966

How: Taking Advantage of Vulnerable People through Contractual Manipulation

Why: Done in Order to Profit From Systematically Extending Slavery

Who: White Farmers

Category: Wealth Prevention

Status: Inactive, Reverberating

Sharecropping began shortly after formal slavery ended and it was designed to keep former slaves and their descendants working for free. Sharecropping was just another ploy to manipulate susceptible and newly freed Black people into generating wealth for white power. Former slaves and others worked in the fields in exchange for a share of the profits generated by the crops. In an issue of *Jet Magazine*, there is an interesting photo of Dr. Martin Luther King meeting with Black sharecroppers in the 1960s to commemorate 100 years of sharecropping. In the photo Dr. King is seen showing a U.S. dollar to shocked sharecroppers with the camera capturing their expressions of disbelief. The descendants of slaves were so exploited that one hundred years after emancipation they had never seen or touched money. The bottom line is sharecropping produced much more fabricated debt than it provided profits. Land owners routinely cheated and trapped illiterate sharecroppers by piling on debt in order to create a cycle of debt and dependency. The only thing this vicious debt cycle did was keep Black sharecroppers toiling in the fields for meager room and board.[43]

What: Colonialism

When: 1880s to Present

How: By Invasion and Forcing Africa into Near Total Submission

Why: To Pillage the Wealth That Africa Would've Used to Develop and Become Competitive

Who: White Europeans

Category: Wealth Prevention and Grand Theft

Status: Reduced to Neocolonialism

In Europe slavery ended in 1833 but after a few decades their massive slave profits started drying up. A few European countries decided the answer was to colonize Africa and through tyranny openly exploit them for their resources. This open form of looting and extortion began around 1881 and formally ended when African nations rebelled enough to gained semi-independence in the 1960s and 1970s. Europeans weren't done ransacking so they consolidated control over Africa's resources by implementing a system of neocolonialism. Today Europe uses economic sanctions and the doctrine of unequal trade—all reinforced with bribes, threats of a coup or assassination for the purpose of remotely controlling their "former" colonies.

Currently Black Africa remains mired in neocolonialism or unofficial colonialism while mouthpieces for white power offer a different narrative to explain African poverty. They ignore 500 years of slavery, 100 years of colonization, current neocolonialism and instead conduct an idiotic comparative analysis with a few successful Asian nations and then fault Black genetics for Africa's misfortunes. Currently white foreigners, both government and corporations oversee and govern nearly every aspect of these African nations' existence including their raw materials and mineral wealth, media, banking, politics and even governments. France is the worse tyrant state as they steal over 400 billion USD annually from their collective "former" colonies.[44]

Chapter Two: How White Supremacy *Kills* Black Americans

Chapter one focused on weapons for controlling Blacks, with death as a secondary control method. This chapter explores deadly medical, chemical, and biological weapons, including a trifecta of lethal tools: homosexuality, abortion, and vaccinations. If Hitler were alive today, he might reconsider his direct approach and opt for these long-term systematic weapons of destruction. Though slower than a gas chamber, these tactics are equally effective in eliminating a group of people from the Earth.

What: The New Birth Control: Targeting Blacks with Homosexuality

When: 1990s to Present

How: Media Bombardment, Academics, Sellouts, Heavy Recruitment, Powerful Reward System, Total Indoctrination, Ignoring Valid Counter Arguments and Force

Why: To Lower Black Fertility Rates, Misdirect Efforts to Secure Black Liberation, Infect Blacks with disease, Emasculate Black Men, divide the Black Populous and Justify Eliminating Black Society

Who: Leftist White Elites, Democratic Party, Corporate America and Related Power Structure

Category: Birth Control, Genocide

Status: Most powerful Genocidal Weapon. Permanent Exemption from Challenge and Above Reproach

Most gay rights supporters conclude that opposition to their lifestyle or agenda is rooted solely in hatred and a phobia. However, few people have ever heard of "cultural colonialism." The fact is people rightfully resent another group reconstructing their existing norms and customs. With that said, it seems that white power wants Black people around the world to adopt its culture and values, while it never wants to respect the preexisting culture and patterns within the group.

To further understand why so many Black people around the world resist the same-sex movement and reject the agenda, and ultimately why Black America is regarded as homophobic, we have to examine the history of white domination and how it works. Cultural colonialism refers to the domination or imposition of one culture over another, often by a more powerful or influential group. It involves the systematic promotion and spread of the dominant culture's values, norms, beliefs, and practices to the detriment or marginalization of the indigenous or subordinate culture.

For instance, white power extended it influence in Africa through a phenomenon called cultural colonialism. The tactic employed various methods and tactics to shape and even force European culture, values, and practices onto African societies. Cultural colonialism served as a vital tool of European powers to assert dominance over African populations. White power successfully colonized Africa thanks to missionary efforts aimed at spreading Christianity and European ideology for the purpose of exerting three-dimensional control over the masses.

The results of this expansion span from genocide to the erosion of African customs and identity. It's important to recognize that culture, defined as the way of life of a people encompassing their ideas, actions, and creations, plays a significant role in determining whether a society progresses rapidly or slowly. Anthropological research consistently demonstrates that a society's traditional values are closely tied to its readiness to accept or reject the demands of modern industrial or commercial endeavors. In today's interconnected world, established cultural norms largely dictate whether a society adopts or opposes innovation and change, as well as the pace at which these transformations occur.

This process can take various forms, including the suppression or erasure of indigenous cultures, languages, and traditions, as well as the imposition of the dominant culture's language, education, religion, and social systems. Cultural colonialism can occur through direct political and military control, economic influence, media and communication channels, and other forms of cultural dissemination.

Cultural colonialism often results in the loss of cultural diversity, identity, and autonomy for marginalized groups, as well as the perpetuation of power imbalances and inequalities. It can have far-reaching social, psychological, and economic consequences, impacting everything from self-perception and community cohesion to political and economic development.

Overall, cultural colonialism represents a form of cultural imperialism, where the dominant culture seeks to assert its dominance and control over other cultures, often at the expense of their cultural integrity and autonomy. When people observe Blacks, they easily overlook that they are discussing a subjugated people, and the many instruments used to maintain that conquered status. When oppressed people complain about something, it is usually a legitimate complaint.

Currently, Black Americans are frequently associated with various aspects of the same-sex movement and culture, including cross-dressing, sexual reassignment surgery, and same-sex marriage. This prompts the question: Given the alphabet movement has its origins in white society, exactly how did Black America become so closely associated with this alternative lifestyle in the first place? Answer, homosexuality is the new birth control. White power is using this alternative lifestyle to commit Black Genocide, which is considered the most destructive and effective way. Any valid criticism is simply ignored, which is a scary fact given that this alternative lifestyle is being used to strategically wipe people off the Earth. Nothing else so incredibly dangerous is allowed the pass given to the same-sex agenda. Same-sex relations and gender-identity issues are controversial and often immune to criticism. Fast-food discussions may touch on obesity and cancer; crack cocaine talks involve potential health risks and legal consequences. Similarly, discussions about gang-banging highlight the risks of arrest or physical harm—not so with the same-sex agenda. Criticizing mass incarceration is acceptable, not so with any aspect of the same-sex agenda. Slavery was devastating but after 363 years of slavery the Black population grew to nearly five million people...but after 363 years of strategically forcing dangerous behavior onto Blacks they are guaranteed to go extinct. Only gay rights has total immunity and is discussed without bringing up AIDS, hepatitis, drug addiction, targeting children, suicide and most of all, *genocide.*

The existence of the Black race will not be jeopardized by an abundance of crack addicts, and sponsoring black-on-black crime alone is insufficient for a complete genocide. White power cannot target small children for mass incarceration or abortions, unlike the same-sex agenda. An abundance of same-sex lifestyles can hinder the standard 2.1 replacement rate required to sustain a population. Its acceptance and capacity for open depopulation, along with untouchable status, positions it as the primary tool for the near complete annihilation of Black America. This assertion is not hyperbole; it is supported by several facts, starting with an examination of the definition of genocide provided by the United Nations (UN).

The UN offers an official definition and criteria for genocide on their sanctioned website and based on that definition, same-sex lifestyles meets several criteria. According to the United Nations Office on Genocide Prevention and the Responsibility to Protect, section Article II.

> In the present Convention, genocide means any of the following acts committed with intent to destroy, in whole or in part, a national, ethnical, racial or religious group, as such:
>
> I. Killing members of the group;
> II. Causing serious bodily or mental harm to members of the group;
> III. Deliberately inflicting on the group conditions of life calculated to bring about its physical destruction in whole or in part;
> IV. Imposing measures intended to prevent births within the group;
> V. Forcibly transferring children of the group to another group.[45]
>
> Forcing or strategically targeting a vulnerable minority group with behavior known to lower birthrates meets genocide criteria, causing harm, creating conditions for physical destruction, and imposing measures to prevent group births. Let's delve into the UN resolution.

Concerning Article II, section A, "killing members of the group" is achieved by targeting a group with a risky behavior linked to a deadly disease. Despite data showing AIDS prevalence in the Black community, white power continues to target the community with the risky lifestyle. The high suicide rate linked to the same-sex community's behavior should be scrutinized, yet opponents of the lifestyle face criticism, and excessive drug usage goes unaddressed in the campaign to indoctrinate and recruit young people.

Article B claims, "causing serious bodily harm to members of the group" constitutes genocide and the high rate of disease, suicide, drug use, and domestic violence does enough damage to meet this criteria.

Article C is what separates it from other deadly vices and truly champions genocide. The rule states, "Deliberately inflicting on the group conditions of life calculated to bring about its physical destruction in whole or in part." It is undeniable that a significant consequence of having an extremely large same-sex population is a decrease in childbirth, as two people of the same sex cannot reproduce.

Article D, "Imposing measures intended *to prevent births within the group*" is also right up the alley of same-sex behavior because everyone knows that same-sex activity lowers birthrate by default—ignoring the fact and disallowing these realities to change the discourse says leftist white people are as much a part of the campaign to lessen the Black population as the far-right. Remember, the author is simply reading the UN definition and trying to determine if in fact, rampant same-sex activity can be linked to genocide.

The conclusive evidence of the catastrophic impact is evident in the census figures. The 2000 United States Census marked a historic moment as the Latino population equaled that of Black Americans for the first time in U.S. history. With each group at 35 million people, both demographics were about 12 percent of the population, with Latinos expected to quickly surpass Blacks. This was significant as Black Americans had been the second-largest racial group after whites for centuries. In the 2020 Census, Latinos numbered 52 million, constituting 18.5% of the US population. Today, the media overlooks the fact that the Black American population only grew by a meager 0.5% to reach 13.4% over two decades. Such a minimal growth rate raises questions about its normalcy. If this rate were to decline to -10.00 percent, the information would likely be dismissed, and the genocidal systems, designed by whites to gradually lower Black birthrates, would remain undisclosed.

If having millions of homosexuals can negatively affect birthrates, and the lifestyle meets four out of five genocidal criteria, are objections to gay rights rooted in common sense for group survival, or are they driven by blind hate and homophobia?

It has been established that while something only has to meet a single UN tenet for being defined as genocide, this particular behavior meets FOUR and is therefore extremely dangerous and easily defined as a form of genocide. This behavior can present a significant danger and easily fits the definition of genocide. In addition to the UN definition, same-sex relations are *biologically* linked to lower birthrates. Here is a concise overview of the issues associated with same-sex behavior.

Drug Addiction. The alphabet community has a longstanding issue with excessive substance use, acknowledged for its lethal impact in a variety of formal and informal circles.

Suicide. Gender and sexuality-related suicides have surged among Black youth, exceeding rates among their white counterparts. It has become a leading cause of death for Blacks, challenging stereotypes about coping mechanisms amid institutional racism. Fast-forward to the present, and a construct created by white individuals (gay rights) has shifted that paradigm, resulting in the tragic deaths of Black individuals as young as five due to "gender identity issues."[46]

Diversion and Misguidance. Black people rarely march for reparations, protest police misconduct, or address black-on-black crime. Rather, they demonstrate over topics like same-sex marriage. The benefits of this foreign transformation for the Black community remain uncertain, as gay rights supporters struggle to identify a single positive aspect when questioned. The author queried dozens of supporters, asking, "Can you name one positive aspect of this lifestyle that outweighs AIDS, suicide, and genocide?" However, no one has offered a response, with many activists acknowledging the absence of a positive aspect to counterbalance the issues of AIDS and genocide.

Angela Davis, a renowned freedom fighter in the 1960s, declared herself a lesbian in 1997, shifting her focus to gay rights. Since then, there has been mostly silence from her on Black issues. The redirection of Black freedom fighters to gay rights instead of Black causes does not benefit the Black community.[47]

Causes Division. White society has proven to be experts at dividing and conquering and gay rights is another way to do so. Since the majority of Blacks don't agree with gay rights the best way to cause division is by sponsoring a behavior that the majority inheritably opposes. It is not lost on the Black community that most black gay rights activists exclusively campaign for same-sex issues and ignore or abandon Black causes. Thanks to white power more and younger blacks are identifying with the homosexual lifestyle and thus guaranteeing a lower birthrate in the future and further ripping apart the already fragile Black family. Many Blacks are rightfully seething at the fact that AIDS is being introduced and normalized through this behavior and movement. The same-sex lifestyle divides black homosexuals who campaign for gay rights from Blacks who fight for Black related issues; it divides the family; it divides Black women from Black men and it divides black homosexuals from the general Black population. That's a lot of division for a group already divided.

Everyone engages in actions that others may object to, but the key difference lies in keeping private matters private to avoid unnecessary conflicts. The overt approach of the same-sex community creates tension as people dislike being confronted with private matters such as questionable sexual behavior. The relentless recruitment of children particularly disgusts many in the general public. Refusing to acknowledge valid opposing arguments, especially regarding the impact of AIDS, is unacceptable.

AIDS and Syphilis. After creating AIDS and targeting a particular lifestyle, the next step was to target Black people with that behavior. Meanwhile, in Africa, white supremacists declared war, directly injecting HIV into unsuspecting Black Africans. The U.S. employed a subtler approach, successfully infecting millions of Black people by targeting them with the infected lifestyle. One doctor in Fulton County, Georgia, claims that a whopping 70 percent of Black women there are infected.[48] The *CNN* claim that AIDS is a black disease is not true and leaves out the real facts. First, in the U.S. there are an estimated 4 million people living with HIV and not all of them are Black. Second, even if all of them were Black that figure, 4 million amounts to less than 10% of Black America, which was counted at nearly 45 million in the 2020 Census. Third, *CNN* omitted that over 75% of the blacks who are infected with HIV were infected through the same-sex lifestyle. AIDS was originally titled GRID, or Gay Related Immune Deficiency. Yet, *CNN* has too much respect for the same-sex agenda to truthfully call AIDS a "gay disease," so they lie on the one group who they apparently do not respect at all, Black America.[b]

It is not just AIDS; 83% of syphilis in the U.S. is found in the same-sex community, along with most hepatitis, gonorrhea, and anal warts. If a food product caused AIDS, the world would be warned to avoid it; if alcohol caused sterility, society would be discouraged from using it. This lifestyle seems to be a hotbed for contagions, and nature is urging abstention. Why does same-sex activity get a pass and is even forced onto society? Sometimes being too politically correct and censoring information can increase health problems. Ever heard of Gay Bowel Syndrome? The reason why you have not is because it is a condition found in the male homosexual community, and it would shine a negative light on that group, therefore it must remain a secret. They also suffer from anal incontinence, anal fissures, diarrhea and lost sphincter control.[49] Lesbians are not safe either, according to the CDC there are over 30 diseases unique to lesbians, and when the author read the article it was difficult to even pronounce most of the conditions. The CDC is no match for the powers of gay rights, as when the author returned to digitally retrieve the article from their official website, it was

---

[b] *Black AIDS Epidemic "AIDS in America Today Is a Black Disease,"* CNN, July 31, 2008, World Star Hip Hop, https://www.worldstarhiphop.com/videos/video.php?v=wshhz6pQ2ysYx5iHM97a

deleted! Apparently that health-related information is expected to remain hidden away like Gay Bowel Syndrome.[50]

Emasculating Black Men. Leftist white power causes far-reaching concerns about targeting fatherless Black boys with images of effeminate Black men. What did Black America do to deserve being targeted with behavior that has no upsides and lowers birthrate? Why not launch a comparable campaign toward communities with robust traditional values and high birthrates? Why not target actual enemies for population reduction lifestyles? Despite U.S. intelligence claims of Russia's interference in a U.S. presidential election and alleged involvement with the Afghanistan Taliban, there is a notable absence of effeminate Russian men advocating for gay rights on American television.[51]

For over a decade, viewers heard, "Coming up after the commercial break, homophobia in the Black community…" After being portrayed as "homophobic" and targeted for change, Black America has become the face of queerness. The media's constant use of black homosexuals in campaigns is questionable, and popularizing this lifestyle to the youth is a concerning path towards potential Black Genocide. Selective aiming makes it clear that a war is being waged against masculine Black men and the Black family, demonstrating that the very survival of Black people is in the crosshairs of leftist white power.

Lower Birthrate. Imagine 20,000 heterosexual men and women desiring solitude on an island, with separate islands chosen by 20,000 lesbians and 20,000 male homosexuals. All islands receive basic provisions. The final outcome in this hypothetical example highlights the significance of heterosexuality and questions the notion of treating same-sex as equal.

If individuals on these islands were aged 18-30, the male homosexual island would likely decline inside 75 years, and the lesbian island in less than 80 years. With all islands getting the same provisions, only the heterosexual island would persist indefinitely. This hypothetical example highlights the importance of recognizing and preserving heterosexuality, contrasting with perceived negative consequences of high same-sex levels.

If an asteroid reduced the global population to 40 people, half of them being homosexuals, repopulating the Earth would be nearly impossible. Finally, any remaining hunter-gather society will be quickly wiped out if they normalized same-sex activity. Despite the genocidal impacts evident in various scenarios, selective amnesia prevails when contemplating the ultimate outcome in a community saturated with this behavior. Its widespread acceptance inherently reduces fertility rates on a mass scale, tantamount to calculated extermination.

Domestic Violence. The media covers domestic violence inside the straight community so often that it comes as a surprise to learn that violence within the same-sex community is worse.[c]

They use unproven pseudoscience and claim "they are born that way."

This claim is a recruitment tool for young people and also serves a purpose to win court decisions. However, every time there is a large scale study on identical twins the results strongly contradict the claim that people are born homosexual. These studies consistently show that one twin is living as a heterosexual and the other is involved in a same-sex relationship. There isn't any "gay gene" so if there isn't any gay gene found in the human body, then it can't possibly be purely genetic.[d]

---

[c] *Is violence more common in same-sex relationships?* Joanna Jolly, November 18, 2014, *BBC News,* https://www.bbc.com/news/magazine-29994648 see also Lesbian Partner Violence Fact Sheet, https://mainweb-v.musc.edu/vawprevention/lesbianrx/factsheet.shtml

[d] *Are People Born Gay?* Jeff Johnson, *Focus on the Family,* https://media.focusonthefamily.com/fotf/pdf/channels/social-issues/16-fotf-0035-545013_spc3_thriving_values_are_you_born_gay_kit_disk-

Taking a look at the list of drawbacks provided, it should be apparent that genocide seeking white power totally benefits from their achievement of popularizing same-sex inside Black America; millions of blacks are drug-addicted-AIDS-infected-no-child-producing-homosexuals. Blacks are divided and embattled with a same-sex civil war along with a measly 0.5% growth rate per twenty years. The concocted lies used to advance the same-sex agenda is easily addressed without any hatred or bias. For example, activists claim "being gay is the same as being Black," but during slavery white supremacists regularly raped male slaves either for fun or during a ritual known as "buck-breaking." Today, there are not any "gay ghettos," and Blacks have the lowest median income while homosexuals have the highest median income in the U.S.[52]

Liberal politicians address same-sex concerns, and police rarely target them with deadly force. Some members of the group use racial slurs, demonstrating their awareness of the distinction between sexuality and race. Others claim "all of us are born gay" but (1) Not all individuals in same-sex relationships assert they were born that way, (2) too many people enter prisons one way and come out another, (3) influential pornography is tempting and has a conversion rate, (4) every study of identical twins destroys the "gay gene" theory with one being straight and the other is not, (5) rarely do small children behave that way without coaching and influence, (6) people often choose to change their sexual preferences back and forth, and (7) this fabricated claim

---

online.pdf?_ga=1.189427179.1785140915.1459272893 and *There is no 'gay gene,' no 'straight gene.' Sexuality is just complex, study confirms,* PBS, August 29, 2019, https://www.pbs.org/newshour/science/there-is-no-gay-gene-there-is-no-straight-gene-sexuality-is-just-complex-study-confirms *Large-scale GWAS reveals insights into the genetic architecture of same-sex sexual behavior,* August 30, 2019, *Science Magazine,* https://science.sciencemag.org/content/365/6456/eaat7693

does not explain or allow bisexuality. It remains unclear how two heterosexual parents can pass down homosexual genes. To deceptive, civilization-destroying activists, any confession that childhood abuse caused same-sex tendencies mean nothing. They argue that this lifestyle is a civil rights issue, but they do not extend civil rights to any sexual behavior they personally find repulsive. Their "open-mindedness" wavers when it comes to legalizing sexuality they consider unfit for mainstream acceptance.

No other issue is so unimpeachable that every single negative factual statement is offensive. If you say "The best way for men to contract AIDS is through same-sex," that is homophobic. "Some homosexuals are racist" is homophobic. "Some homosexuals don't like heterosexuals" is also homophobic. "Homosexuality doesn't reproduce" is connected to homophobia instead of tied to biological genocide.

Disenchanted white Americans can return to Europe, unhappy Blacks to Africa, and miserable Mexicans can go back to Mexico for a better life. If the same-sex community is unhappy and desires genuine equality, why not create their own state or island? Reluctance hints at sustainability concerns, opting instead to destroy heterosexually built societies.[53]

Their reluctance to establish an autonomous society suggests an awareness of the inherent flaws in their reproductive model. When society regulates to prevent that same collapse, they cry discrimination. Their hesitation to create their own nation stems from fear of failure, yet they oppose regulatory measures for self-preservation, branding it as bigotry.[54] Rather than forcing societal conformity to a behavior that can threaten extinction, why not establish independent states? Answer: A "gay state" cannot endure without recruiting other people's children. Hence, they prefer enlisting children, altering restroom norms, and imposing severe penalties for symbolic acts of dissent such as burning a rainbow flag.[55]

Instead of passing rules that forbid calling a man wearing a skirt a man they should start their own independent nation.[56] Same-sex relations has been on Earth thousands of years and never recorded both a majority and long lasting society or state, and when historians discuss the previous empires that a large homosexual population brought down they are called....you guessed it, homophobic. Something innocent like suggesting that human sexuality should be discussed between parents and students at home can get a teacher fired.[c] With the help of shortsighted and gullible blacks this white sponsored ticking time bomb is guaranteed to singlehandedly reduce the Black population to rubble within 300 years.

The power of same-sex community lies in the incorrect taxonomy that it enjoys. To advance an agenda they demonize dissent and label all opposition "homophobic" while hiding behind claims of equality. It is spoken alongside race and gender issues instead of being in other categories such as deviant sexual behavior that society frowns on, or on a genocidal list of weapons used by white supremacy to control birthrate and infect a chosen group with a deadly disease. People change their sexual behavior all the time but they do not change their gender or racial identity nearly as often.

This behavior's inability to sustain a society does not make it entirely inferior. In some historical contexts, homosexuals might appear successful in head-to-head competition with heterosexuality. However, this victory is short-lived, as it does not allow humanity to endure. A unanimous decision should suggest that either heterosexuality must prevail or face extinction. In the 1980s, AIDS disproportionately

---

[c] *New Jersey School Board Member Who Denounced LGBTQ Curriculum Resigns After Zoom Incident,* Tara Mahadevan, November 26, 2020, https://www.yahoo.com/entertainment/jersey-school-board-member-denounced-183404347.html

impacted the same-sex community due to their high and incomparable promiscuity. In the same-sex community, homosexuals were openly promiscuous, while heterosexual men faced some societal judgment for their comparatively lower numbers of sexual encounters. Same-sex culture tends toward promiscuity and drug use, while heterosexuality is considered superior for building and maintaining civilization. Heterosexual values encourage abstinence until marriage, contrasting with the early sexual engagement endorsed in the same-sex community.

The same-sex community has public bathhouses and lounges facilitating instant anonymous sexual encounters, while gay bars are known for serving hard liquor to minors.[57] Despite these factual critiques, the incorrect taxonomy with race and gender renders all of negative facts as homophobic.

Heterosexual family parades are child-friendly and modest, while certain same-sex parades involve nudity and explicit displays with children in attendance. Parks mostly frequented by heterosexuals generally avoid obscene public sex acts, unlike some parks dominated by homosexuals.[58]

These undeniable facts are presented without fear of or hatred toward any individual. It is fitting for everyone to be cordial, including towards members of the rainbow community. Being mean-spirited based on sexual preference is unacceptable. However, the concept of a "perfect world" with an equal mix of heterosexual and same-sex individuals is unrealistic and *naturally* would inevitably lead to self-destruction. The so-called phobia is not against individual persons; it arises from the assured decline of essential heterosexuality, inevitably leading to the demise of civilization. Those who dismiss these views as irrelevant or discriminatory, lack any substantive responses to these significant and truthful drawbacks.

Widespread same-sex activity and long-term societal sustainability have nothing in common. Ignoring the impending decline and criticizing those who oppose depopulation is abnormal. This point is rightfully underscored in this book that links Black American history to Black Genocide. Unfortunately, political correctness has silenced individuals, leading them to overlook the deteriorating consequences of unchecked practices. With white power heavily targeting Blacks with a same-sex agenda, they are scheduled to be the first impacted and deleted. If this book is stating facts, yet the genocidal effect of widespread same-sex behavior cannot be extensively discussed in a book about group survival, then where can it be?

Here are ten reasons why some people despise gay rights, and it has nothing to do with homophobia. (1) Using media and propaganda, politics and corporate America, activists pummel society with their agenda and reconfigure every single institution ranging from the church to the military. (2) Activists are constantly hijacking words or inventing new and annoying terminology or acronyms, and if anyone fails to use them then they are considered offensive or homophobic. (3) There is not a single upside for any group that is overrun by same-sex behavior—only eventual destruction due to a lowered birthrate. (4) Activists infamously and routinely target other people's children. (5) Many people frown on using pseudo-science to redefine "male and female," or spread falsehoods like "we are all born this way" and "we're the same as Blacks." (6) ALL factual, constructive arguments are completely censored and considered hate-speech with no exceptions. (7) Supporters avoid linking "AIDS" and "homosexuality" or addressing how it is employed to control population size. Instead, they present same-sex behavior as completely harmless. (8) Rampant same-sex behavior has historically and effectively helped destroy advanced societies in the past, and that was before life-shortening AIDS. (9) Most heterosexuals find it unsettling that many same-sex individuals automatically reject the opposite sex. Lesbians and homosexuals boast about being uninterested in the opposite sex for intimacy or companionship. While demanding an "open-minded" attitude towards them, they often harbor dislike and rejection towards the opposite sex.

(10) Hollywood, a biased supporter, aggravates opponents with its radical endorsement. In biopics like Madam CJ Walker's, they inaccurately introduce the lifestyle for the sole purpose of advancing the same-sex agenda in historical narratives.[59] Envision an unhindered, gay rights agenda propelling society towards unavoidable ruin – throughout history, unchecked same-sex has consistently confronted and defeated heterosexually built civilizations, guaranteeing long-term population decimation for those societies. Supporting gay rights aligns with a trajectory leading to the collective demise of society, placing advocates on the wrong side of history.[60]

What: Abortion and Black Infant Mortality

When: 1970 to Present

How: By Locating Clinics near Blacks, Offering Complicated Speech and Sophisticated Explanations to Gullible Black Leadership, Imposing Litmus Tests

Why: To Critically Lower Black Birthrate

Who: Leftist White Brokers of White Supremacy

Category: Genocide

Status: In Full Effect, Code-BLUE—Loss of Consciousness

In some cities in the United States the abortion rate exceeds the birthrate for Black society with estimates of three out of four babies being aborted is Black. The majority of these population control facilities are within walking distance of Black areas.[61] A well-written article in the *Wall Street Journal* titled *Let's Talk about the Black Abortion*

Rate discusses how for years in New York the Black birthrate was lower than the abortion rate. Here are the facts that prove another weapon is being used to reduce the size of the Black population.

> Abortion impacts African Americans at a higher rate than any other population group. In 2011, the Centers for Disease Control and Prevention released an Abortion Surveillance Report. According to that report, Black women make up 14 percent of the childbearing population. Yet, 36 percent of all abortions were obtained by Black women. At a ratio of 474 abortions per 1,000 live births, Black women have the highest ratio of any group in the country.
>
> When you use those percentages, it indicates that of the over 44 million abortions since the 1973 Roe vs Wade Supreme Court ruling, 19 million Black babies were aborted. African Americans are just under 13 percent of United States population. White women are five times less likely to have an abortion than Black women. Perhaps it is a matter of availability. A study by Protecting Black Lives, in 2012, found that 79 percent of Planned Parenthood's surgical abortion facilities are located within walking distance of minority communities.
>
> In the past, we criticized the tobacco industry for targeting young people with their advertising. Recently, the nicotine vape industry has been criticized for similar practices. The prevalence of abortion providers in African American and Hispanic neighborhoods indicates the abortion industry is targeting too. It smacks of the eugenics-linked past of Planned Parenthood founder Margaret Sanger and her views of contraception and abortion as ways of diminishing the black population.
>
> The impacts on our Black communities are hard to fathom. According to the Guttmacher Institute, which generally supports abortion, in 2011 360,000 Black babies were aborted. CDC statistics for 2011 show that 287,072 Black deaths occurred from all other causes excluding abortion. By these numbers, abortion is the leading cause of death among Blacks.

> That same year, Dr. Kermit Gosnell, an abortionist in the Philadelphia area, was arrested. His arrest followed a raid on his clinic by the Drug Enforcement Administration. Agents were acting on suspicion that he had been over prescribing Oxycodone, but once inside the clinic, they were shocked to find female patients writhing on tables, in a facility that was littered in feces from a flea-ridden cat that could roam free inside the premises. Dr. Gosnell was eventually charged with murder of a woman that had died from a botched abortion, and for several "live birth" abortions where he had killed babies born-alive. It is outrageous that it took a drug raid to finally bring the authorities to look at this house of horrors.
>
> You would think such a horrific occurrence would be a big news story. When he went to trial, the press gallery was empty. Kermit Gosnell's abortion mill was in a Black community. The news media did not care.[62]

Every demographic has people who automatically contribute to birth control without the targeting and interference from another group. There are people who purposely decided to limit the size of their family or even forgo having children for financial and personal reasons. There are others who have been told that medical reasons or physical problems prevent them from reproducing. Those members of a given community already offer a counter-balance to over-population yet white society sees itself fit to decide on whether or not those people are enough to regulate the size of a population. What is unknown to most people is that based strictly on the history of abortions and its eugenic origins, if there wasn't any Black African slavery in the U.S. then there wouldn't be an abortion industrial complex. Based on the timing and the profiles of those who financed and legalized abortion that claim is undeniable. White supremacy concluded that if Blacks were not going to continue to be slaves then they might as well be dead, and abortion was born. Neutered black leadership allows white power to easily omit this incriminating documented history and that omission is essential to any long-term open purge operation.

A fair examination of the original person who presented abortion as a way to lower birthrate is a good way to understand how we got where we are today. Margaret Sanger is credited with coining the term "birth control." She was a staunch eugenicist who wrote and spoke openly about normalizing abortion to limit the size of families. For years she worked as a nurse in low-income neighborhoods and her observations moved her to conclude that criminals, prostitutes, mentally ill and others were the products of being in a family with too many children. The original name for abortions was "The Negro Project" with Sanger calling Black people "human weeds."

Great challenges remain for Black babies lucky enough to avoid abortion and survive gestation. Thanks to systemic racism infant mortality rates for Black babies are higher than any other demographic with no improvement in sight. Here are some excerpts from think tank American Progress:

> Racism is the one constant toxin contributing to the maternal and infant mortality rates of Black women. According to the iconic anthropologist Ruth Benedict, in her 1945 seminal work Race: Science and Politics, she describes racism as "the dogma that one ethnic group is condemned by nature to hereditary inferiority and another group is condemned by nature to hereditary superiority." Centuries of subjugation, by individuals and systems have created a toxic environment for African Americans, especially African American women.

They also posit:

> In addition, research reveals that discrimination produces negative results on one's overall health indicators. According to Michael Lu and Neal Halfan, authors of *Race and Ethnic Disparities in Birth Outcomes: A Life-Course Perspective*, the constant wear and tear of racism

on Black women's bodies can manifest later in life, compounding with stress to negatively affect maternal and infant health outcomes.[63]

In addition, Keisha Bentley-Edwards, co-author of "*Fighting at Birth: Eradicating the Black-White Infant Mortality Gap*," states that "particularly for Black women, despite age, educational attainment and socioeconomic status, the exposure to racial inequities and injustices throughout their life directly impact their birth outcome." The world should know that Bill Gates and the Gates Foundation have donated nearly 100 million dollars to pro-abortion organizations.[f]

What: Dangerous Vaccinations

When: 1940s to Present
How: Schemes, Deceit, Denial and Mystery Medicine

Why: To Control Select Populations

Who: White Controlled Pharmaceutical Companies, Alleged Philanthropists and Governments

Category: Population Control

Status: Active, Covert

---

[f] *Obama awards abortion activists Bill, Melinda Gates,* November 25, 2016, *One News Now,* https://onenewsnow.com/science-tech/2016/11/25/obama-awards-abortion-activists-bill-melinda-gates Warren Buffet and his wife donated well over 2.5 billion dollars to pro-abortion organizations, see *Maafa 21—Black Genocide in the 21st Century,* Documentary, February 22, 2018, *Live Action,* YouTube channel, https://www.youtube.com/watch?v=I6XfU8KVkzI

Some of the staunchest proponents of Black Genocide are found in the vaccination arena because they realize that one of the best ways to reduce populations is through unsuspecting inoculation programs. Bill Gates is reputed to use vaccinations in order to sterilize, paralyze and even euthanize people all over the world. For many people Gates established himself as a population controller when he stated, "First, we've got population. The world today has 6.8 billion people. That's headed up to about nine billion. Now, if we do a really great job on new vaccines, health care, reproductive health services, we could lower that by, perhaps, 10 or 15 percent." With a background in computer software instead of medicine, and a penchant for predicting virus outbreaks before they happen, Gates is considered so notorious for depopulation that some politicians openly suggest he should be arrested for crimes against humanity.

Sara Cunial, a member of Parliament described Gates as a "vaccine criminal," and publicly urged the Italian government to arrest Gates and turn him over to the International Criminal Court so he could be tried for crimes against humanity.[64] Days earlier, an intercepted human intelligence report revealed Gates offered a $10 million bribe to a Nigerian official to force a mandatory Covid-19 vaccination program. The interest in vaccinating Africans for the Wuhan Virus was expressed before there was a serious outbreak in Africa and long before there was a proven vaccine available. Even his wife, Melinda Gates favors exterminating Black people "first." Bill Gates was interviewed on CNN and Anderson Cooper asked:

> In terms of who gets the vaccine first, your wife, Melinda Gates, said that, this week that health care workers should get the vaccine first. And then she said, quote, "It's also going to be Black people who really should get it first and many indigenous people…" [65]

Bill Gates agreed. Here are excerpts from an article provided by *Genocide News* which describes the impact that Gates' vaccinations have had on Black people:

> In 2010, the foundation funded a phase 3 trial of an experimental malaria vaccine that ended up killing 151 African infants and leaving more than 1,000 with severe adverse effects like paralysis and seizures. A similar campaign in Sub-Saharan Africa, the 2002 MenAfriVac effort involving the forced vaccination of thousands of African children, left 50 kids paralyzed. A few years later, the WHO was accused by the Catholic Doctors Association in Kenya of chemically sterilizing millions of women in that country via their tetanus vaccine campaign. Lab tests revealed that every vaccine tested contained a sterility formula, and the WHO later admitted it had been developing sterility vaccines for more than a decade.
>
> It's also worth noting that a 2017 study found that the popular DTP vaccine from the World Health Organization was killing African children at an alarming rate, with DTP-vaccinated girls experiencing 10 times the death rate of kids who had not been given the vaccine. At a time when the left is so quick to label anyone or anything imaginable as being racist – including *milk* – it's interesting that no one is calling out the Gates' foundation on their comprehensive and frighteningly well-funded efforts to accelerate the depopulation of Black people.[66]

At 35-years-old Prince William, second in line to the British throne, warned that exploding populations were putting enormous pressure on wildlife and urgent depopulation measures were needed. He stated, "In my lifetime we have seen global wildlife populations decline by over half." At the gala dinner for the Tusk Trust charity in London, he continued:

> "We are going to have to work much harder, and think much deeper, if we are to ensure that human beings and the other species of animal with which we share this planet can continue to coexist. Africa's

> rapidly growing human population is predicted to more than double by 2050—a staggering increase of three and a half million people per month. There is no question that this increase puts wildlife and habitat under enormous pressure."

The Prince added:

> "Urbanization, infrastructure development, cultivation—all good things in themselves, but they will have a terrible impact unless we begin to plan and to take measures now." [67]

Once again someone white has shown their affinity for animals and utter disregard for Black people. There are persistent allegations that vaccinations laced with the HCG hormone have been used in Mexico, Nicaragua, Tanzania, Kenya and the Philippines. The HCG hormone causes women's bodies to reject and abort their fetuses leading to miscarriages.[68]

Here are the known facts concerning the tetanus vaccination campaigns in Mexico, Philippines and Nicaragua:

- Only women were vaccinated, and only the women between the ages of 15 and 45. In Nicaragua the age range was 12-49. Even though men are as likely as young women to come into contact with tetanus they were excluded. Children were also excluded meaning only women of child-bearing age were vaccinated.
- Human chorionic gonadotrophin (HGC) hormone has been found in the vaccines. HGC is not normally found inside tetanus vaccines.
- The vaccination protocols called for multiple injections—three within three months and a total of five altogether. But, since tetanus vaccinations provide protection for 10 years critics wonder why multiple inoculations were required.

- The first response of the World Health Organization (WHO) when confronted with the presence of HGC was denial followed by a claim that it was a false positive.
- WHO has been involved in the development of an anti-fertility vaccine using HCG tied to tetanus vaccinations for over 20 years.

According to *Vaccine News* even flu shots are known to cause spontaneous abortions.

> A CDC-funded medical study being published by the medical journal *Vaccine* has confirmed a shocking link between flu shots and spontaneous abortions in pregnant women. The study was rejected by two previous medical journals before *Vaccine* agreed to publish it, further underscoring the tendency for medical journals to censor any science that doesn't agree with their pro-vaccine narratives.
>
> "A study published today in *Vaccine* suggests a strong association between receiving repeated doses of the seasonal influenza vaccine and miscarriage," writes CIDRAP, the Center for Infectious Disease Research and Policy. "A puzzling study of U.S. pregnancies found that women who had miscarriages between 2010 and 2012 were more likely to have had back-to-back annual flu shots that included protection against swine flu," reports Medical Xpress, a pro-vaccine news site that promotes vaccine industry interests.[69]

White power is so open about exterminating Blacks that French doctors publicly suggested that vaccination programs to combat the Wuhan Virus, Covid-19 should begin in Africa, even though at the time Europeans were being hammered by Covid-19 while very few Africans were suffering from it![70] Scientists have also blown the whistle about governments placing contraception in water and food. In 1969 *The New York Times* printed an article titled *A Sterility Drug in Food is Hinted,*

Biologist Stresses Need to Curb Population Growth. The article detailed efforts to put contraceptives in food and water to control populations.

The CDC is considered a criminal organization by many scientists aware of their role in developing harmful vaccines and concealing that danger from the public.[71] In 2014, it was discovered that a measles vaccination called the MMR vaccine was causing autism in Black children 340% more often than in white children.[72] The information was covered up 13 years earlier by the CDC when they published an article claiming it was safe and the vaccination was used. The fraud was so troublesome that one CDC researcher, Dr. William Thompson broke ranks and contacted Dr. Hooker, the father of a vaccine injured child, and confessed to being a part of the cover up. Over the course of numerous recorded conversations with Dr. Hooker, a remorseful Dr. Thompson admitted the CDC knew in 2001 the vaccine was linked to autism yet deliberately covered up the findings.

Through emails, Dr. Thompson provided the father compelling evidence by sharing restricted CDC memos never meant for public scrutiny. The classified CDC data sheets made it clear they knew Black boys were known to be at a much higher risk for autism from the MMR vaccinations. Dr. David Lewis, an international expert in whistle blowing and the detection of scientific fraud, reviewed the original CDC documents which admitted the link to autism and compared them with the fabricated CDC documents that claimed the vaccine was safe. He stated, "Probably this is the clearest case and the easiest case in which to answer is this fraud or is it an accident, is it just an artifact of the study that we are dealing with here, clearly it is fraud."[73]

Meanwhile, according to Project Censored, "Since 1988, the U.S. Government has paid $3.2 billion to 4,150 individuals and families for injuries and deaths attributed to shots for flu, diphtheria, whooping cough, and other conditions." How far are mad scientists willing and able to go? The U.S. Government investigated if the Pentagon weaponized ticks and created Lyme disease. A *Newsweek* article reported, "Last week, the U.S. House of Representatives quietly passed a bill requiring the Inspector General of the Department of Defense to conduct a review into whether the Pentagon experimented with ticks and other blood-sucking insects for use as biological weapons between 1950 and 1975."[74]

This book was written at a time when vaccinations were being developed for the pandemic caused by the Chinese Wuhan virus. Should anyone Black receive the injection? Let's see, white people flooded Black areas with crack-cocaine, spiked public water supplies with birth control drugs and toxins, invented AIDS, forced the AIDS infested lifestyle on Blacks, carry signs that say "black trans lives matter" more than black transsexuals do and do not do that for any other group, have medicine commercials that shows Blacks happy to be HIV+, executed the Tuskegee Experiment, perform sneaky compulsory sterilizations on Black women to this day, disproportionately locate liquor stores, fast-food and abortion clinics in Black areas, target Blacks with tobacco, finance violent rap music that kills Black people, and have the nerve to want Blacks to be the first to get a rushed and unproven vaccination full of mystery drugs. This white resume should convince any sane Black person to strenuously fight and reject any vaccination developed by white power.

What: Eugenics and Compulsory Sterilization Programs

When: 1890s to Today

How: Through Court Decision, Deceit and Coercion

Why: To Lower the Birthrate of Select Groups

Who: U.S. Government, Wealthy Whites and the Eugenics Board

Category: Population Control, Genocide

Status: Inactive, Reverberating

To understand compulsory sterilization one must first understand eugenics. A common definition of eugenics is,

> The study of how to arrange reproduction within a human population to increase the occurrence of heritable characteristics regarded as desirable. Developed largely by Francis Galton as a method of improving the human race, it fell into disfavor only after the perversion of its doctrines by the Nazis.

The eugenics movement started in the 1890s and was funded by wealthy white elites such as the Carnegie Foundation, John D. Rockefeller and other plutocrats. Today, wealthy white people like Warren Buffet and Bill Gates continue this legacy of funding targeted population control. The goal of making eugenics a legal reality happened after a landmark Supreme Court decision. The 1927 case of *Buck v. Bell* is infamous for Justice Oliver Wendell Holmes's offensive conclusion: "Three generations of imbeciles are enough." By a vote of 8 to 1, the Supreme Court allowed the forced sterilization of Carrie Buck by the state of Virginia. Buck's was the first of thousands of such sterilizations in the state before the practice was ended in 1974. Virginia's stated intent was to prevent Buck, already a single mother, and the others from conceiving "genetically inferior" children. *Buck v. Bell* was a great legal victory for the American eugenics movement which strove to perfect the "race" and "white" civilization.

The administrators of white supremacy used the legal decision to sterilize men and females as young as nine years old. The victims were usually women, poor, incarcerated, accused of mental illnesses, American Indians and Latinos. Black women bore the brunt of this racist movement and it was routine to fabricate reasons or use deception to sterilize vulnerable citizens. Michelle Oberman, author of *Thirteen Ways of Looking at Buck vs Bell* cautioned that,

> Using the word "state" or "Virginia" allows for too much anonymity. It was a "cadre of earnest, self-righteous, and occasionally delusional individuals"—lawyers, politicians, doctors, and others who thought they were doing good—who instituted a system that surgically sterilized tens of thousands against their will or, as in the infamous "Mississippi appendectomy," quite deceptively. Their victims were poor, disproportionately women, and often women of color.[75]

In the 20th century, state governments deemed 70,000 Americans unfit to reproduce and forced them to undergo mandatory sterilization. Almost half of the controversial medical procedures occurred in just three states: California, North Carolina and Virginia. Most states administered forced sterilizations through their state governments and targeted prisons, mental asylums and welfare recipients. North Carolina went further and empowered social workers to decide who was eligible for forced sterilization, resulting in 7000 cases, second only to California with 20,000 such cases. To date Virginia and North Carolina have paid compensation to the victims.[76]

In North Carolina, the compensation effort hit a wall when Republicans took control of all branches of government in 2011. "You just can't rewrite history," said the late Republican state Sen. Don East. "I'm so sorry it happened, but throwing money don't change it, don't make it go away. It still happened." Senator East was among those who openly feared that giving compensation to sterilization victims would open the door to other reparations claims. To finally persuade Republicans to support restitution the compensation movement offered to limit the funds to living victims only, and exclude the families of dead ones. Those were the terms for the compensation funds included in the budget signed into law by Republican Governor Pat McCrory in 2013. It applied to all victims who were alive at the time of the signing with payments starting one year from the signing of the bill, another attempt to drag it out and wait for more victims to die off.

Periodically, judges offer Black people sterilization in exchange for lighter sentences. In Tennessee a judge offered inmates the opportunity to reduce their sentences if they agreed to sterilization. The judge claimed he was trying to encourage "personal responsibility" so inmates won't "be burdened with children" when they are released. The judge stated "This gives them a chance to get on their feet and make something of themselves… I understand it won't be entirely successful but if you reach two or three people, maybe that's two or three kids not being born under the influence of drugs. I see it as a win-win." The problem is contraception does not prevent drug use or provide income. Forcing Black women to be sterilized remains a reality in 2020. A PBS documentary titled, *Belly of the Beast* revealed that between 1997 and 2014 nearly 1,400 women were forcibly sterilized in California prisons, most of them Black.[77]

What: Feeding Black Babies to Alligators

When: 1800s to 1920s

How: By Kidnapping and Killing Black Babies

Why: Pure Evil

Who: White Men

Category: Genocidal Tendencies

Status: Inactive, Clean Getaway

Throughout history, savage members of the white oppressor race have been deliberately callous in rendering barbaric treatment to the most vulnerable Black people, including infants. Such was the case when white men used Black babies as lure for hunting alligators. During slavery, the 1800s, and post-slavery, numerous instances recount white men using Black infants and toddlers as alligator bait. Placed on riverbanks, these small children were used to lure alligators out of the water. The alligators would often consume these infants, and at times, the babies were pre-killed and even skinned for bait. The practice is described in the following passage:

> Alligator baiting was very popular in the 1800-1900s. The skins were used to make shoes, bags, belts and other items. However, white hunters often lost their arms and sometimes their lives as they rustled the swampy waters at night attempting to attract alligators to the surface, so they decided to use slave babies as bait. This horrendous act was later characterized in sheet music, postcards and figurines.

Despicable white men, the personification of evil, opted to use Black babies instead of chickens, dogs, goats, pigs, or fish as alligator bait. In the Florida region, the common practice of tying Black babies to a rope and feeding them whole to alligators is well-documented and available in various forms, some of which are archived at the Jim Crow Museum of Racist Memorabilia in Michigan.[78]

What: Tuskegee Experiment

When: 1932 to 1972

How: By Taking Advantage of Illiterate Sharecroppers and Unsuspecting Black Military Personnel by Withholding Medical Treatment for a Deadly Venereal Disease

Why: No Value for Black life

Who: The U.S. Government

Category: Genocidal Tendencies

Status: Inactive

From 1932 to 1972, the U.S. Government conducted the Tuskegee Experiment at the Tuskegee Institute, now Tuskegee University. Participants, mostly uneducated sharecroppers and military men unaware of the experiment, were promised free medical care. Initially monitored for "bad blood," a term used for various medical conditions, the patients were not informed of their participation. In 1947, when penicillin was found effective for syphilis, the doctors chose to monitor rather than treat the patients. During this period, at least 28 men died from syphilis, 100 from related causes, and 40 wives were infected, with 19 children born with congenital syphilis.

The CDC ended the experiment not due to its medical apartheid, unethical nature, or cruelty, but because a whistleblower exposed it to the press. Despite the common belief among Black Americans that the Black patients were injected with syphilis, they were only monitored and left untreated. Throughout history, white power has often found support from black individuals in efforts to harm Black society. Eunice Rivers, a black nurse, served as the coordinator for the Tuskegee Experiment from 1932 to 1972. Aware that infected Black patients were not receiving medical treatment, Rivers recruited 399 victims, and received top recognition and awards from the white masters she served. Many Black historians view Eunice Rivers as the ultimate race traitor.[79]

What: Creating AIDS

When: Unleashed in the Late 1970s

How: Created in a Lab during the 1970s, Spread through Vaccinations, and by Promoting the Same-Sex Agenda mostly to Blacks

Why: To Control the Black and Homosexual Populations, and Reap Profits from Killing Blacks

Who: U.S. and South African Governments

Category: Population Control, Genocide

Status: Inactive, Mission Accomplished

While studying the AIDS virus some medical investigators have spent years researching additional issues like government funding for biological weapons programs involving viruses, as well as key individuals related to known labs and such programs. Many scientists who deeply probed into the origins of HIV have concluded that AIDS was manufactured in labs in the United States during the 1970s. According to Leonard Horowitz, author of *Emerging Viruses*,

> "In 1969 . . . [the] United States Defense Department requested and got $10 million to make the AIDS virus in labs as a political/ethnic weapon to be used mainly against Blacks. The feasibility program and labs were to have been completed by 1974-1975; the virus between 1974-1979. The World Health Organization started to inject AIDS-laced smallpox vaccine into over 100 million Africans (population reduction) in 1977. And over 2000 young white male homosexuals (Trojan horse) in 1978 with the hepatitis B vaccine through the Centers for Disease Control/New York Blood Center. . . ." [80]

Strike one: AIDS emerged suddenly, seemingly out of nowhere. Strike two: Despite widespread and diverse sexual activity across demographics, AIDS exhibited selective impact, affecting some more than others. Strike three: The original and dubious narrative blamed

Africans and Haitians for eating monkeys, a story inconsistent with the limited contact between rural Africans and major cities—making it implausible to infect millions across the continent with HIV. Once again, white power, mirroring the crack epidemic strategy, counts on mere denial, leveraging the challenge of tracing attacks without irrefutable evidence. The Republican initiative to eradicate Black communities evidently utilized both chemical (crack) and biological (AIDS) agents. Ronald Reagan and George Bush maliciously deployed a bioweapon, coinciding with the introduction of crack cocaine. AIDS, like crack, offered white power a windfall of benefits, stigmatizing select demographics and reducing their population through fatalities. The U.S. and France exploited impoverished Africa, profiting billions by charging for their patented HIV test and instilling mass hysteria to prompt expensive testing across Black Africa. The underwriters of white supremacy designed AIDS to bolster resistance to miscegenation by stigmatizing Blacks. Beyond its devastating impact on Black lives, AIDS generates billions in ongoing revenue through the sale of permanent medications to combat the disease.

Speaking of video recorded confessions, a former member of South Africa's apartheid-era intelligence service, in a documentary called *Cold Case Hammarskjöld*, shockingly confessed on camera that the AIDS virus and other diseases were intentionally spread among the population to eliminate as many Blacks as possible. Alexander Jones, a key member of the South African Institute for Maritime Research (SAIMR), aimed to hinder majority Black rule in South Africa by injecting AIDS into unsuspecting Blacks in neighboring countries under Keith Maxwell's command, with the goal of permanently consolidating white rule. As reported in *The Guardian*:

> Keith Maxwell wrote about a plague he hoped would decimate Black populations, cement white rule, and bring back conservative religious mores, according to papers collected by the film-makers. Maxwell had no medical qualifications but ran clinics in poor, mostly Black areas

> around Johannesburg while claiming to be a doctor. That gave him the opportunity for sinister experimentation, Jones says in the film… A sign advertising "Dokotela [doctor] Maxwell" still hangs from the side of an office in Putfontein where locals remember a respected man with a virtual monopoly on the area's healthcare. [81]

The film primarily centered on the mysterious 1961 plane crash of former UN secretary-general Dag Hammarskjöld near Ndola, Zambia. During the investigation, the filmmaker uncovered Alexander Jones, who openly admitted on camera that SAIMR, with support from the CIA and British Intelligence, employed fake vaccinations to disseminate the HIV virus in the South African Development Community. Jones conveyed to the filmmakers, "We were at war. Black people in South Africa were the enemy." SAIMR was connected to the nation's infamous chemical and biological warfare (CBW) program, overseen by Dr. Wouter Basson. This program served apartheid racists in covert efforts to harm Black populations in South Africa and beyond.

Dr. Basson, nicknamed Dr. Death, oversaw the use of chemical and biological warfare (CBW) against South African freedom fighters and the public. Leaders in South Africa, Angola, and Namibia alleged the use of dangerous chemicals for crowd control, evident in the region's significantly higher AIDS rate compared to other parts of Africa. Throughout the 1980s, Basson was involved in attacks and assassinations of anti-apartheid activists and he provided death squads like SAIMR and the Civil Cooperation Bureau with lethal chemicals to use against the general public. When F.W. de Klerk became president in 1990, he ordered the production of CBW's be stopped and the lethal agents destroyed. Subsequently, Basson focused on legal drugs and non-lethal chemicals, including a substantial quantity of ecstasy, which he supplied to drug dealers in anti-apartheid communities. His arrest in 1997 during a sting operation in Pretoria revealed he possessed 1,000 ecstasy tablets.

On July 31, 1998 Basson appeared before the Truth and Reconciliation Commission and provided testimony for 12 hours. The

Commission determined that Basson had been the primary decision maker in the highly classified bioweapons program, Project Coast, and therefore should be put on trial. Basson faced 67 charges, including theft, drug possession, drug trafficking, fraud and embezzlement, 229 murders and conspiracy to murder. After a 30 month trial he was acquitted of all charges. Basson went on to established businesses in the South African private sector and became a multi-millionaire.

In the 1980s, Project Coast, a covert South African government program, aimed to disassociate the government from chemical and biological weapons CBW attacks. Additionally, it explored methods to control the Black birthrate. Roodeplaat Research Laboratories began as an animal research facility but later expanded to investigate chemical and biological warfare agents.[82]

Daan Goosen, Roodeplaat Research Laboratories' founder, told the British Broadcasting Corporation that Project Coast supported a secret contraceptive project for use on the Black population. Goosen stated the project had devised a "vaccine" for both genders, and researchers were exploring covert delivery methods. Evidence at the Truth and Reconciliation Commission suggested attempts to introduce birth control substances into water supplies. Project Coast, funded by the U.S., South Africa, and Britain, parallels the questionable CIA program MK Ultra. Independent research into MK Ultra reveals such potentially racist programs within white-controlled governments.[83]

The compelling evidence lies not in written records or explicit confessions but in the significant number of Black casualties. In the U.S., promoting harmful lifestyles to a vulnerable group achieved the intended outcome. In Africa, AIDS is more prevalent in regions with a large Black population and less common in North Africa, where predominantly white colonizers reside. The suddenness and selectivity speak for themselves. The tailored nature of HIV, despite millions of interracial relations, demonstrates the artificial origins of AIDS.

Chapter Three: How White Supremacy *Controls* and *Kills* Black Americans

The first chapter discussed various weapons employed to control Blacks, some incidentally lethal. The second chapter focused on more direct weapons intending to reduce the Black population, with some surviving the assault. This chapter features the different ways that white supremacy actually controls and kills by using a combination of tactics. Brokers of white supremacy realize that control mechanisms and killing apparatuses can be combined into a single force in the name of protecting white interest. This chapter includes containment measures that can and often does lead to death, giving Blacks no other alternative but to be controlled to death. Whether death is incidental or was the focal point, being controlled to death suits the purveyors of white supremacy just the same.

What: Crack-Cocaine

When: 1980s to Present

How: By Aiding the Contras to Import Megatons of Drugs into the United States

Why: To Finance Foreign and Domestic Interests While Killing, Disfiguring and Incarcerating Blacks

Who: CIA, U.S. Government, Contras and Black Street Gangs

Category: Chemical Warfare, Genocide

Status: Active

In an orchestrated move, several major U.S. cities with substantial Black populations were inundated with a new drug, crack-cocaine. Notably, cities in the Midwest and Pacific Northwest, lacking a large Black population, initially remained unaffected. The government insists on requiring video evidence and confessions for proof of a chemical attack, yet executing such a widespread and targeted operation is nearly impossible for an individual or organization. Upon the U.S. Government's initial introduction of crack-cocaine to Black America, some perceived it as a targeted assault, akin to genocide, well before its devastating impact unfolded. In their 1990 report, The State of Black America, they stated, "There is at least one concept that must be recognized if one is to see the pervasive and insidious nature of the drug problem for the African American community. Though difficult to accept, that is the concept of genocide." [84]

The coordinated, nationwide introduction of crack unmistakably demonstrated its deliberate use to harm Black citizens, prompting subsequent political investigations. The Reagan Administration, Justice Department, and CIA vehemently opposed inquiries led by Senator John Kerry. They minimized their drug dealing activities in public statements, employed delaying tactics, dismissed evidence, urged media attacks on the hearings, financially devastated investigative journalists, harassed and intimidated witnesses, withheld documents and evidence, actively obstructed testimony, and issued death threats. Several individuals, both inside and outside the U.S., lost their lives while seeking information or talking to the press.

With all of this government obstruction, there was still overwhelming evidence discovered by Kerry's team. On page 14 of his epic book, *Dark Alliance*, Gary Webb penned:

> Kerry and his team had taken videotaped depositions from Contra leaders who acknowledged receiving drug profits, with the apparent knowledge of the CIA. The drug dealers had admitted—under oath—giving money to the Contras, and had passed polygraph tests.

> The pilots had admitted flying weapons down and cocaine and marijuana back, landing at least on one instance at Homestead Air Force Base in Florida. The exhibits included U.S. Customs reports, FBI reports, internal Justice Department memos.[85]

The Kerry Committee's report, titled, *Drugs, Law Enforcement, and Foreign Policy*, strongly criticized and found "substantial evidence of drug smuggling" involving individual Contras, Contra suppliers, Contra pilots, mercenaries associated with the Contras, and Contra supporters. Robert Parry expressed the following:

> Kerry's report was issued two years later, on April 13, 1989. Its stunning conclusion: "On the basis of the evidence, it is clear that individuals who provided support for the Contras were involved in drug trafficking, the supply network of the Contras was used by drug trafficking organizations, and elements of the Contras themselves knowingly received financial and material assistance from drug traffickers. In each case, one or another agency of the U.S. Government had information regarding the involvement either while it was occurring, or immediately thereafter."
>
> The report discovered that drug traffickers gave the Contras "cash, weapons, planes, pilots, air supply services and other materials. "Moreover, the U.S. State Department had paid some drug traffickers as part of a program to fly non-lethal assistance to the Contras. Some payments occurred "after the traffickers had been indicted by federal law enforcement agencies on drug charges, in others while traffickers were under active investigation by these same agencies." [86]

Launching this chemical weapon benefited white power by justifying the "war on drugs," causing mass incarceration and unemployment. The drug's impact on newborns, termed "crack babies," suppressed birthrates, and resulting mass imprisonment contribute to a genocidal impact, while also fueling prison slave labor. Crack aids the purveyors of white supremacy in disrupting families, causing addiction, and fostering mental health issues. The police, key players in the far-right strategy, accumulate billions through forfeiture assets, and contribute to the killing, terrorizing, and mass incarceration of Black people. Crack fuels black-on-black crime, linking the Black image to drugs and violence, ensuring frequent police encounters. Hollywood profits from showcasing distorted images of Blacks, while white power capitalizes on cultural normalization and popularizing drug sales through rap music, boosting the prison system. It is a jackpot for white power.[87]

What: Chattel Slavery

When: 1502 to Present

How: By Force

Why: To Exploit Black Labor for Nation Building

Who: The U.S. Government and White Society

Category: Control and Genocide

Status: Inactive, Reverberating

The Arab Slave Trade stands out as the most severe form of chattel slavery due to its use of castration to control slave populations. According to Bernard Lewis, author of *Race and Slavery in the Middle East*, Islamic law required medical care, proper maintenance, and lifelong support for slaves. White Arabs practiced slavery from 600 CE to the 1960s, and it persists today. Contrary to common belief, slavery did not start in the U.S. in 1619.

A successful slave revolt in 1526, known as San Miguel de Gualdape, in what is now Georgia, proves that slavery occurred in the

United States well before the commonly cited date of 1619. European (Spanish) introduction of slavery in 1502 was followed by this rebellion, marking the first instance of former African slaves living free in the New World. With chattel slavery officially ending in 1865, it lasted for 363 years, not accounting for other forms like sharecropping.

For over 300 years, Africans generated trillions in wealth and constructed nations for others. The term "chattel" denoted not only being someone else's property but also being treated akin to farm animals. In a historical shift, slavery spanned from birth to death, devoid of religious protections or church oversight. The Atlantic Slave Trade, infamous for its brutality, involved rape, torture, and bondage, serving as a means to build empires.

Chattel slavery may have ended, but modern slavery persists in the U.S., taking both direct and subtle forms. Subtle slavery occurs when employers exploit vulnerable individuals by compelling overtime without proper compensation, often affecting powerless illegal immigrants. Direct slavery is evident in the U.S. prison system, currently utilizing cheap prison labor, a constitutionally allowed exception. Incremental racism contributes to the procurement of Black inmates by judicial systems. Blacks face disproportionate encounters with police, higher arrest rates for minor offenses, increased likelihood of prosecution, higher conviction rates, harsher sentences, and lower chances of parole compared to others.[88]

What: Convict Labor Leasing

When: 1880s to Present

How: By Passing Laws That Allowed the Re-Enslavement of Blacks and Place Them into Brutal Prison Camps

Why: To Profit from Extending Slavery and Undermine Liberation

Who: Southern States

Category: Slavery Extension to Generate White Wealth

Status: Active

After the abolition of slavery, some European nations turned to colonizing and exploiting Black Africans for economic gain. While the United States did not engage in African colonization, a system of convict labor leasing was implemented, taking advantage of Black Americans for economic purposes. After slavery formally ended, Black Americans, including former slaves, actively pursued success in various aspects of life. In the Deep South, over 2,000 Black Americans held political offices at various levels shortly after the abolition of slavery, contributing to political, economic, and social life. Driven by envy, scheming, suit-wearing race guerillas initiated a fresh form of subjugation.

The U.S. Constitution banned slavery but included a loophole, allowing individuals convicted of a crime to be treated as slaves while in prison. Southern states quickly exploited this, establishing a sinister program known as convict labor leasing. This system involved creating laws to ensure a continuous influx of inmates for free labor, extending the legacy of slavery. After chattel slavery ended in 1865, laws like Pig Laws and Black Codes enabled the legal arrest of Blacks for minor or non-existent offenses. These laws allowed white power to legally arrest and incarcerate Blacks for nothing or minor violations.

Criminalizing petty offenses like sidewalk spitting, vagrancy, and cursing disproportionately targeted Blacks, leading to a surge in arrests and incarcerations. For decades, this legal exploitation fueled the prison population, sending armies of innocent Black men into forced labor on railroads, coal mines, plantations, and quarries. Alabama employed convict leasing from 1846 to at least 1921. According to Douglas

Blackmon in his book, *Slavery by Another Name*, by 1883, convict labor leasing contributed to 10% of the state's revenue, rising to 73% by 1898. Through free labor, southern states and American corporations generated hundreds of billions of dollars in profits.

After conviction, inmates endured exceptionally harsh forced-labor conditions, surpassing the brutality experienced by many field slaves during slavery, and arguably standing out as the most barbaric mistreatment in U.S. history—both inside prison and otherwise. Garbage food was thrown onto the ground the same way a zookeeper feeds wild animals and inmates caught taking a bath were severely beaten. Being permanently shackled in some way or fashion was the norm. Institutional slavery had paternal protections and relationships that developed over many years of interaction between slaves and slave holders. Without paternalism the prisoners were routinely killed by labor or disease, remained in the same clothing for years, ate slop buzzards would not eat, slept on the concrete ground on a piece of cardboard and woke up with a mandate to perform over half a day of dangerous backbreaking work. In 1873, an estimated 25% of the Black convict laborers were worked to death.

Convict labor leasing re-enslaved almost 200,000 Black men, generating hundreds of billions for white-owned businesses and state governments. Its economic success transformed the system into a standard prison procedure, rather than being phased out. According to a *Newsweek* article, prisoners in Alabama, Arkansas, Florida, Georgia, Texas, South Carolina, and Oklahoma receive no payment for their labor in government-run facilities. With over two million individuals incarcerated in the U.S., nearly forty percent are Black. On average, inmates earn .14 cents per hour, while the highest-paid inmates receive .63 cents per hour nationally. Based on percentages, there could be nearly one million disenfranchised and over-sentenced Black people still working in the labor leasing programs today.[89]

What: Violently Establishing and Maintaining Sundown Towns

When: From about 1890 to 1980s

How: Violence

Why: Jealousy, Economic Lockout, and a Desire to Purge Blacks from Land and Keep them Poor

Who: Defeated Confederates, Ku Klux Klan, Vigilantes, Police

Category: Genocidal Tendencies, Wealth Prevention

Status: Active

After emancipation, freed slaves enthusiastically migrated to various corners of the United States for a new beginning. The 1870 U.S. Census shows that free Blacks were recorded in the farthest reaches of every state.[90] In contrast to common belief, many rural white Americans welcomed and coexisted peacefully with these industrious newcomers. In just a few years, these hardworking freedmen took on roles as blacksmiths and carpenters, and some even set up their own farms and businesses. After the Civil War, confederate sympathizers and the newly-formed Ku Klux Klan undermined fledgling Black settlers by attacking and lynching them in the countryside. From about 1890 onward, these militias set fire to farms and homes, looted businesses, stole their land, and lynched between 5,000 and 10,000 Black men.[91]

Ethnic cleansing turned these towns all-white, marked by racist signs prohibiting Blacks with warnings like "nigger, don't let the sun shine on you in ___." This violence compelled many Blacks to move to cities, seeking refuge from expulsion. Decades later, elderly survivors recounted childhood memories of fleeing lynch mobs into the woods with only the clothes on their backs.

Thousands of white-only sundown towns still exist, and today the white residents claim to only oppose certain Blacks perceived as problematic. However, successful Blacks pursuing socioeconomic equality were violently targeted, facing resistance from banks, realtors, and police. The last racist sundown signs were removed in 1981.[92]

What: The Destruction of Black Wall Street

When: 1921

How: Violence

Why: Jealousy and Insecurity

Who: White Vigilantes, Law Enforcement

Category: Wealth Prevention

Status: Dissolved, Reverberating

Currently and by design, there are no designated economic centers specifically built by and for Black America. Historical patterns reveal that Black economic advancement alone can incite animosity from advocates of white power, prompting violent responses. Notably, in Tulsa, a group of Black investors defied considerable odds to establish the prosperous Greenwood district. One major investor was J.B Stradford who moved to Greenwood in 1899 to purchase various land vacancies in the area. After buying these vacant lots he insisted on selling them exclusively to other Black residents for development into residential houses and businesses. This strategy flourished, leading to the establishment of Black Wall Street—a diverse array of businesses, homes, and professionals, including wealthy families with airplanes. In 1921, amid jim crow and within 60 years of slavery's end, J.B. Stradford became one of the wealthiest Black Americans, owning numerous properties in Greenwood, including his own hotel, The Stratford Hotel.

Greenwood's incredible success fueled jealousy in white Tulsa. Violence erupted over a false accusation of a Black man assaulting a white woman. After his arrest, white vigilantes gathered at the jail to lynch him, prompting armed Black men to intervene, resulting in gunfire. That episode and pent up jealousy sparked hate-fueled attacks that led to the total destruction of Black Wall Street in what amounted to the worst race massacre in US history. Blocks of Black owned businesses were firebombed from airplanes while the sheriffs indiscriminately armed and deputized angry white men who then murdered, and looted, and burned down nearly everything in sight.

When the holocaust ended nearly 300 Blacks were killed, over 800 people were admitted to surrounding hospitals, almost 10,000 were left homeless, 1,256 residences were destroyed, and 600 successful businesses were lost including 21 restaurants, 30 grocery stores, two movie theaters and a hospital.[93] As with any atrocity, white America does not feel obligated to either apologize or compensate the survivors and their heirs for the billions of dollars that was lost in generational wealth.

What: The Destruction of Rosewood

When: 1923

How: Violence

Why: Jealousy, Hatred and Insecurity

Who: Vigilantes

Category: Wealth Prevention

Status: Dissolved, Reverberating

History shows that sacking prosperous Black sections of town is not rare in American history. Two years after white jealousy demolished the Black economic zone in Tulsa they struck again in Rosewood Florida. In 1923 someone falsely claimed that a Black man attacked a white woman resulting in the formation of a white lynch mob. They went about Rosewood burning and plundering while killing several residents. Fearful of retaliation, the Black residents refused to fight the vigilantes and instead hid in the swamps for days. One courageous man, Sylvester Carrier took up arms and killed two white men before being slain in a shootout. Word traveled that two white men were killed and hundreds of armed white men from all over the state joined the lynch mob already in Rosewood.

Blacks established a thriving self-sufficient community in Rosewood, complete with churches, homes, stores, and a timber industry, all maliciously annihilated to crush any prospects of upward mobility. The death toll ranges from 6 to 27 Blacks, with two whites killed. Despite no arrests, the state of Florida compensated the surviving victims with two million dollars in 1997..[94]

What: The Destruction of Slocum, Texas

When: 1910

How: Violence

Why: Hatred and Insecurity

Who: Vigilantes

Category: Racial Violence

Status: Dissolved, Reverberating

About a decade before Greenwood, a furious white mob in Slocum, Texas, massacred an estimated 100 to 200 Black men, women, and children, with historians uncertain about the motive. The reasons range from a Black man owing money to a white man and refusing to pay, to a Black farmer supervising white men in road maintenance, violating white supremacy. Additionally, the attack could have been connected to celebrations of Jack Johnson's historic boxing victory over Jim Jefferies, which triggered attacks on Blacks nationwide.

In Texas, proponents of white supremacy exhibited brutal and deadly actions towards Blacks. Texas was notorious for lynching Black men with little or no reason. For instance, on March 3rd, 1910, during Allen Brooks' trial for allegedly assaulting a white child, a white mob stormed the Dallas courtroom, dragged him out, and promptly hung him from a nearby light pole. Local newspapers praised the mob for swift justice, criticizing the courts for "delays, reversals, and failures."

Months later, on July 29th, hundreds of Black men, women, and children in Slocum were killed while trying to escape racial atrocities perpetrated by marauding white men. In the Slocum Massacre, Black citizens were discovered deep in the woods, shot in the back as they attempted to flee the unprovoked violence. Over two days, armed white men systematically looted, burned cabins, and killed Blacks on sight, marking a tragic episode in history. These savages seized the land and belongings of Black residents and for decades, the state of Texas, along with media and schools, overlooked the incident. Despite the presence of a marker acknowledging the event, white residents contested its placement, asserting, "If nobody was ever arrested, then it never happened."

The ushers of white supremacy love to advise Blacks to pull themselves up by their bootstraps. But urban renewal, red-lining, sundown towns, Greenwood, Rosewood and Slocum demonstrate the drastic extent sponsors of white power will go to in order to completely disenfranchise Black society. It also shows how successful Black America would be if they were simply left alone. To recap, contemptuous white supremacists, from the president of the United States to the lowest foot soldier have exhibited an unparalleled yearning to contain Blacks at all costs.

These efforts include recruiting fellow blacks to oppress their own, violently dismantling thriving Black communities without reason, engaging in redlining, and deliberately constructing highways to destroy successful areas. Never before has a group been so resolute in hindering growth and undoing progress for a vulnerable community that has not historically harmed them. The U.S. avoids employing violent measures against peer competitors like Russia or China in its quest for global dominance, unlike the harsh tactics used against Blacks. Their ability to fight back and inflict high casualties is enough to guarantee safety from such dastardly attacks restricted to the Black community. In other words, white America does not mess with others who can adequately fight back, and they themselves could not endure a tiny teaspoon of what they do to Blacks, the true trademark of a notoriously insecure, no chin having, punk-ass bully.

The atrocities in Slocum, Rosewood, and Black Wall Street are not isolated incidents. Research into the "Red Summer of 1919" reveals similar racist attacks by white mobs on Black military personnel and towns across the U.S. Where are these white aggressors today? They persist today, seen in protests against Black Lives Matter, displaying confederate flags, participating in groups like the KKK or Aryan Nation, identifying as alt-right, white nationalists, or conservative. They are media pundits, politicians, and blue-collar workers. They brandish firearms, shoot peaceful protestors, acquit police in Black killings, engage in online racism, deface murals, media figures, and even ascend to the U.S. presidency. If they were alive in the early 1900s, they would have supported destroying Slocum, Rosewood, and Black Wall Street.[95]

What: Internment Camps: The Devils Punchbowl

When: 1865

How: By Forcing Former Slaves into Internment Camps

Why: To Prevent Freedom and Integration

Who: Union Soldiers

Category: Holocaust

Status: Inactive

Few may know about freed slaves allegedly forced into internment camps. In Natchez, Mississippi, after emancipation, the Black population surged from 10,000 to 120,000. Union soldiers compelled the newly freed to live in camps where many died from labor, disease, starvation, and lack of clean water. In a year, over 20,000 perished. Conditions were so dire that some begged to return to plantation slavery. Discussing this disgraceful camp is as overlooked as addressing white Jewish death camps in mainstream media.

If true, obviously this ugly chapter in American history is deliberately ignored. Considering the pervasive genocidal white resume there were likely numerous heinous concentration camps used to kill Blacks, now hidden away from public scrutiny.[96]

What: Deadly Law Enforcement

When: 1704 to Present

How: By Being Granted Special Powers to Detain and Incarcerate Black People by Any Means Necessary

Why: To Protect White Suburbs from Integration, Assist Terrorist Hate Groups, and Enforce Racist Laws while Killing/Maiming and Incarcerating Black People

Who: Slave Catchers, the U.S. Government and Uniformed White Infantry Race Soldiers with Badges

Category: State Sponsored Racial Violence and Re-Enslavement

Status: HIGHLY ACTIVE—Code Red, National Emergency

Few ponder the genesis of policing. Contrary to common belief, American law enforcement is a relatively recent concept. Early police were often unpaid volunteers, and as recently as the 1970s, policing was not a lucrative career. Today, it offers good pay and benefits, typically requiring only a high school diploma rather than higher education. In order to understand the behavior of law enforcement today, we must consider its true origins. Author Sally E. Hadden sums up law enforcement this way:

> "The history of police work in the South grows out of this early fascination, by white [slave] patrollers, with what African American slaves were doing. Most law enforcement was, by definition, white patrolmen watching, catching, or beating black slaves." [97]

Law enforcement's history spans over 160 years of patrolling, surveilling, capturing, detaining, frisking, beating, and returning runaway slaves to plantations. Today, police duties echo these actions, involving patrolling, surveilling, capturing, detaining, frisking, beating, apprehending, and incarcerating individuals. The tools have evolved from slave-catchers using chains and leg-irons to modern police using handcuffs and restraints. Just as historical slave patrols crushed slave uprisings, contemporary police disrupt peaceful civil rights protests. Between 1704 and 1861, slave catchers wielded nearly unchecked police authority, with slave patrols serving as the main law enforcement entities to suppress rebellions, enforce slave codes, and apprehend runaways.

During the Civil War (1861-1865), the Confederacy faced a manpower shortage, prompting many slave catchers to enlist. Consequently, the confederate army assumed policing and slave apprehension duties. Although slavery and slave patrols ceased after the Civil War, American law enforcement was still evolving. In the post-Reconstruction era (1866-1960s), ex-Confederate soldiers, the KKK, former slave catchers, and similar white individuals joined the fledgling law enforcement sector, with local police continuing the work of the original slave catchers. They aided and abetted racist terror groups to repress Black citizenry, and enforced segregation laws to paralyze Black liberation. Decades after Reconstruction ended, (1950s-1980s) routine law enforcement duties expanded to include voter intimidation, union busting, arresting or shooting innocent and unarmed Black taxpayers, destroying organizations with operations like COINTELPRO, suppressing peaceful civil rights rallies, harassing and murdering civil rights advocates, protecting white womanhood, and preventing integration by aggressively patrolling all-white suburbs.

The institution of slavery is also the birthplace of the institution of policing with law enforcement's greatest value being their vital contribution to mass incarceration; with over one million Blacks imprisoned it's also the next best thing to plantation slavery. Thanks to that racist inauguration the culture of racism was ingrained in law enforcement over 150 years before the U.S. developed it.[98]

Chapter Four:
How White Power *Controls* and *Kills* Africans

Space constraints prevent delving into detailed accounts of all African genocides by the French, Germans, Portuguese, Belgians, and white Arabs—which merits its own book. This chapter spotlights weapons systems upholding neocolonialism and explores incidental deaths. It showcases how white supremacists downplay actions, focus on the end results they have produced, while emphasizing derogatory labels like "shithole" countries for African nations.

What: African Oppression

When: 600CE to Present

How: By Using a Variety of Mechanisms Combined With Hard and Soft Power to Eternalize Exploitation for The Purpose of Restricting Africa to a Mere Resource Colony

Why: Originally Used Africans to Build Nations, Currently Depleting African Resources Critical to Maintaining the European, Asian and American Way of Life

Who: The World, White Governed Nations, mostly White Europeans

Category: Wealth Prevention, Genocide

Status: Active

White Arabs predated white Europeans in African enslavement, land seizure, and appropriation of innovations and religion. Having taken territories like the Middle East and North Africa from Africans, white Arabs currently possess swiped African history, stolen Islamic religion, and trillions of dollars from the mineral wealth extracted from Black Africans. White Arabs' historical mistreatment of Black Africans arguably surpasses that of white Europeans. However, the continual international ethnic cleansing efforts by white society draw the most attention.

What is more egregious: white Arabs misappropriating land, religion, culture, and credit for ancient innovations while erasing Africa's original presence in North Africa and the Middle East, or white Europeans and Americans establishing enduring systems to exploit resources and control African prosperity, relegating the continent to a resource colony? Limited space prevents an in-depth exploration, including Africans' forced sale of raw goods. This chapter will focus on some weapons used to dominate Africa and impede development. In no particular order, here is a list of tools used to control and harm Africans.

1. **Assassination and Coups**. Under neocolonialism, African leaders, due to a desire to improve economic conditions and living standards, often face assassination or overthrow. France, in particular, has been implicated in the assassination of at least 22 African leaders and the sponsorship of numerous coups.[99]

2. **Corruption**. Corruption has several templates, but there are two types of corruption that should be discussed. One involves collaboration with external entities like foreign governments and corporations, and the other being organic corruption carried out solely by Africans. Organic corruption may include practices like police shake-downs targeting pedestrians. Large-scale corruption, involving billions of dollars, often requires external assistance, as Africans may struggle to

navigate complex processes such as depositing large sums in foreign banks without foreign help.

At the very top of the corruption pyramids are the foreign governments that misappropriate the most money, which can be trillions of dollars. When it comes to corruption and theft in Africa, pinpointing the top culprit and establishing precise metrics pose challenges and can be difficult. France's colonial tax system is estimated to accumulate at least $400 billion annually by withholding income generated by African minerals and controlling the monetary affairs of 14 formerly colonized African nations.[100]

3. **Systemic Racism**. The IMF, World Bank, UN, and NATO face accusations of promoting white power and racism. The World Bank, exempt from U.S. affirmative action laws, lacks workforce diversity, with only four Black employees out of 3,500 in 2008. These jobs shape policies to uplift poor nations, but the racial bias in employment raises concerns, especially for Africa. If the racism is immeasurable for Blacks seeking employment, what does that mean for Africa? The World Bank is predominantly staffed by "conservative white people," leading to lawsuits by minorities seeking fair employment.[101] African leaders frequently criticize the IMF and World Bank for bias economic policies, drawing complaints even from China and Russia..[101]

4. **Economic Sanctions**. Africans are sanctioned over trivial reasons like a refusal to embrace the alphabet lifestyle, or alleged mistreatment of a group, or an election with a final result that white power condemns. The U.S. and EU should be heavily sanctioned for the gross mistreatment of their Black and brown citizens and the Black Taxes they impose. Since the number one goal of white hegemony is to oppress and manipulate Black people—Africa is sanctioned far more than any other continent. When researching YouTube videos to see what explanations people were giving for Africa being underdeveloped, the all-white cast of content providers and commenters blamed African leaders, geography, corruption, skin color, being mentally inferior, and

weather. Out of hundreds of submissions, not a single white person found on YouTube expressed any of the facts listed here, and they scoffed at slavery and colonialism as reasons for African poverty.[102]

5. **Brain Drain**. By causing so much misery and making parts of Africa unbearable to live, one byproduct is outsiders being able to shake Africa down for their best talent, a strategy known as "brain drain." The African Union estimates that each year over 70,000 African professionals go to other countries and help develop those nations. Most of this valuable talent ends up in the United States and the UK. Based on that figure nearly a million Africans representing specialized manpower resources leave the continent every ten years. Undoubtedly such a workforce could help transform Africa by developing profitable commercial business infrastructures, if only they remained in Africa.

Who wouldn't pursue a better income, improved quality of life, and the ability to support their family? Valued for their skills, Africans are sought after by foreign governments facing shortages of engineers and healthcare professionals. Even Donald Trump, known for his harsh views on immigration, approves the legal entry of thousands of Black African professionals into the U.S.[103]

6. **Colonial Taxes**. France uses a colonial tax system to continue colonizing their "former" colonies. To fully comprehend how outrageous this colonial tax is people need to know the history and tenets of it.

According to African author Mawuna Remarque Koutonin,

> "When Sékou Touré of Guinea decided in 1958 to get out of (sic) french colonial empire, and opted for the country independence. The (sic) french colonial elite in Paris got so furious, and in a historic act of fury the (sic) french administration in Guinea destroyed everything in the country which represented what they called the benefits from (sic) french colonization."

To suppress full independence, the French destroyed Guinea extensively—farms, livestock, equipment, hospitals, roads, libraries, bridges, railroads, and more. After assassinating Sékou Touré, other colonies opted to pay a colonial tax, ceding control of their mineral wealth and governments. France now profits globally from oil and minerals despite lacking these resources domestically.

With media only showing their opulence and high living standards while ignoring France is wealthy from strong arm embezzlement, France is internationally respected and even revered. Whereas other European colonizers phased out their activity in their former colonies to various degrees, France remains dependent and deeply entrenched in every aspect of African affairs. France is completely hooked on the colonial paradigm and unable to advance without having Africa under their draconian control. Currently this neocolonial control is enforced through a tax system requiring those African nations to adhere to the following tenets:

1. Permanent colonial debt for the benefits of France colonization.

2. The automatic confiscation of national reserves with France keeping 85% and giving 15% to the former colonies. France also dictates how the 15% is to be used by the former colonies.

3. Right of first refusal on any raw or natural resource discovered in the country.

4. Priority to French interests and companies in public procurement and public bidding, which gives France complete control on every domestic asset and all construction projects.

5. Exclusive right to supply military equipment and train the country's military officers, which gives France complete control over their militaries.

6. Right for France to pre-deploy troops and intervene militarily in the country to defend its interests.

7. Obligation to make French the official language of the country and the language for education.

8. Obligation to use France colonial money FCFA. This tenet was somewhat successfully challenged. The former colonies are able to use their own currency and banking system but the currency is printed by France and France still has to approve of any spending.

9. Obligation to send France annual balance and reserve reports.

10. Renunciation to enter into military alliance with any other country unless authorized by France.

11. Obligation to ally with France in situation of war or global crisis. Over one million Africans served France in the war against Nazism and Hitler.[104]

After World War II, France's African colonies contributed to European and French reconstruction, with billions from The Marshall Plan. Today, France holds over $500 billion from these contributions, supplemented by annual inflows. Africa provides them with most of the proceeds they get from every asset and mineral ranging from the sale of precious metals like gold to resource minerals like oil, timber, and even food. France also enjoys billions of dollars in profit from displaying the countless stolen artifacts that are now featured in museums all over France.

Italy regularly complains about France continuing to colonize Africa and they point out that if France didn't continue to colonize African nations then France would be the 15th largest economy instead of among the first. That excludes the billions of dollars that France charged Haiti for successfully revolting against slavery.[105]

Excluding mind control, the most effective neocolonial weapon former colonizers use is France's "colonial tax" system. The open secret on the continent is that much of Africa would thrive without France's relentless exploitation of West Africa. As long as West African nations are under this tax system, they will never fully recover financially or mentally from the initial colonization. After all, neocolonization is essentially an extension of the original colonization. It is no coincidence that France's "former" colonies dominate the top ten lists of poorest African nations.[106]

7. **Transferring the War on Terror to Africa**. For centuries, white Arabs waged religious wars in Africa, aiming to divide and conquer for white Arab dominance. Often, this led to having a light brown-skin Muslim leader in Africa, evolving into a white leadership over time. North Africa exemplifies the end results of this tactic, detailed in Chancelor Williams' epic book, *The Destruction of Black Civilization.* Today, white Western power employs its version of this weapon through their "War on Terror" to destabilize Africa.

Most of the 9/11 hijackers were from oil-rich Saudi Arabia, and although Africa was uninvolved in the terrible attack, it was selected as the location for the continuation of that permanent conflict. The move is designed to destabilize African governments, and provide an excuse for foreign militaries to be on the continent in order to secure and control resources. The U.S. alone has admitted to at least 60 military bases in Africa and France is not far behind.[107]

8. **Landlocked Nations**. Globally, most landlocked nations face economic challenges, lacking the competitiveness of countries with ports. There is an old saying among landlocked nations, "When you have a port you serve the world, when you don't have a port, you serve your neighbors." Modern-day African borders, drawn by colonizers, not only resulted in landlocked countries but also perpetuated conflicts between historic enemies who began fighting over lost territory. To understand the issue, imagine another country conquering the Americas, redrawing every boundary line, renaming Mexico, the U.S., Canada, and others, fueling ongoing disputes.

After uniting and overthrowing the conquerors, these nations would still grapple with defining their borders, likely leading to prolonged conflicts and potential landlocked outcomes. If the clashes involve pre-existing adversaries, the strife could persist indefinitely. This encapsulates just a fraction of white power's destructive consequences in Africa.[108]

9. **The Business of Charity**. There is much debate on the charity business in Africa. Charity has long been used as a weapon to undermine African governments through a variety of ways. Countries all over the world have received charity at some point in time, but only Africa receives permanent charity, whether they like it or not. Even when Africans leaders do not want charity they still get charity. Here is just one example of weaponizing charity. Charity can start out with good intentions as mostly white citizens all over the world send aid to an African country suffering from famine.

They see famine and horrible images of starving babies, and millions of whites respond by sending some heartfelt aid. But oftentimes they include items unrelated to the crisis, creating a dependency trap. For instance, during a famine, sending blankets, clothes, shoes, and umbrellas does not address hunger. Agriculture is just one sector; believe it or not, but the African country might have had a successful textile industry during the famine. But no business or sector is able to compete with FREE aid, so consequently the incoming goods end up completely ruining the existing business sector.

After free aid undermines pre-existing companies and sectors they must lay off employees and shutdown, with those people now looking for free food from charity. The textile industries in some of these African nations employed over 5000 people who then go out and helped stimulate the economy, benefitting hundreds of thousands of other people. This happens more often than the public realizes and a great documentary titled *Poverty Inc* attempts to publicize this problem. After collapsing local clothing industries other countries like the U.S. develop secondhand sectors where instead of Africans producing their own merchandise they are forced to buy the same items secondhand from the U.S. They are even banned from manufacturing their own uniforms for law enforcement and military personnel. The agreement heavily favors foreigners, and Africans end up receiving only a fraction of what their own textile industry was making, all because of the onslaught of excessive and unnecessary aid. Readers should know that all of this is planned before it happens.

Getting out of these arrangements is not as easy as getting in. Kenya has been receiving secondhand clothes from the U.S. for years. Some Kenyans are making a good living, and many citizens like the price they pay for the quality they get. But the Kenyan government realizes that the money and jobs being generated from buying and selling secondhand clothes is only a fraction of the profits and jobs once enjoyed by the country's own private sector.

When Kenya and several African nations realized they are earning only a fraction of what they use to make with their own industries, they sought to end the secondhand trade and reestablish their own textile sector. What happened? Donald Trump publicly warned Kenya, Tanzania and Rwanda that their actions constituted a threat to U.S. national security. It shouldn't be lost on anyone that this "threat" is based on producing pants and underwear, not bullets or bombs. Trump followed up that warning with the threat of economic sanctions designed to cripple those African nations. Only Rwanda decided they would not be bullied and went forward with ending the secondhand trade to develop their own local economy. Kenya and Tanzania both backed off and continue to allow an unwanted secondhand clothing trade.

Another problem with endless charity is the mental damage that it does to Africans. Many Africans develop numerous complexes like seeing the white man as superior or a savior while remaining disconnected from having a high-achievement attitude. Many African's inferiority complex is derived directly from the never ending poverty and the endless charity that follows but never seems to solve it. The ramifications of these inferiority complexes are far too vast and prevent completely covering it without a team of professionals and decades of study.[109]

10. Wildlife Propaganda. The ways in which leftist white power oppresses Africa is more subtle but equally effective. By now everyone is use to seeing large migrating packs of animals roam all over Black Africa. If one is hunted the typical mainstream media response is to play violin music and talk about how intelligent the animal was. To understand how the custodians of white power use animals to keep Africa poor let's take Zimbabwe and the elephant. This intelligent and oversized animal is beloved and requires vast roaming areas consisting of hundreds of miles. One way to prevent African nations from developing is to insist they maintain large herds of elephants that number in the hundreds of thousands. African nations face strong condemnation for wanting to develop the open areas where millions of wild animals currently roam because that would require them to do exactly what white nations did and hunt the animals off the land.

How would the U.S. function with millions of wild animals walking around as they please? Zimbabwe President Mugabe made some valid points in addressing the outside pressure to leave the animals in place of development. Mugabe started allowing tourists to hunt the animals to make money and clear the land at the same time but was roundly condemned by white outsiders. Mugabe underscored that big cities everywhere generate much more wealth for a country than safaris do. During a televised speech Mugabe said white governments were using animal preservation propaganda to keep his country poor and he pointed out that he made repeated offers to the UK and the U.S. to take a few hundred of these animals free of charge and relocate them to their countryside. He noted that none of the countries who objected to Zimbabwe's development strategies took him up on his offer and they declined to demonstrate how to best deal with migration and poachers. A large herd of elephants casually roaming through the streets of Los Angeles or London is unacceptable but somehow the same standard doesn't apply to Africa.

Mugabe also said that Zimbabweans loved elephants more than outsiders and didn't need any instructions on how to manage them. He stated Zimbabwe only wanted about 5000 of the 50,000 elephants they had. And that is only one type of animal roaming Zimbabwe. Only in Africa are large herds of elephants allowed to trample important crops, kill farmers, eat the same food as locals, leave large mounds of dung with flies and attract poachers while roaming on land needed for development. With nearly 500,000 elephants, white people also object to Africa setting up large animal reserves because the animals are so numerous no reserves can possibly contain all of them. African nations must also keep their borders open to allow the migrating packs to travel, a natural national security breach to say the least. Images of wild animals roaming with endless dirt terrain support the notion of Africa being a primitive "dark continent."

There would be more white fallout if Mugabe killed 40,000 elephants than if he killed 40,000 Zimbabweans. It is only because of white power and value systems which places wildlife over African-life that allows wide open undeveloped land to be exclusively occupied by animals. There is not a single such large tract in Europe or America where animals have such precedence over human development.

Africans cannot sell the animals, cannot cull them and cannot even give them away to others who say they care so much about them. Apparently to some paleface leftist foreigners a bear family cannot freely roam their city streets or occupy American land slated for development; but an elephant can do so in Africa because the life and well-being of elephants are more important than that of poor Africans wanting to improve their lives. Currently Zimbabwe is being sanctioned into ruin because Zimbabwe had the nerve to confiscate stolen farmland from white farmers and return it to Black farmers. Zimbabwe took the ill-begotten land from white farmers and were sanctioned by white power, then returned it in hopes to have sanctions lifted, and when that didn't work they offered the white farmers over three billion dollars in reparations too. None of that worked and the entire country faces destruction over the well-being of a tiny white minority.[110]

As anyone can see the current condition of Africa is due to so-called white supremacists sacking Africa and using various systems to prevent the continent from reaching its potential because that potential equates to world dominance. The average white person might not be aware of past Black greatness but white governments certainly are; factual and flattering ancient historical texts, innovations and artifacts reflecting Black greatness currently reside in their museums and libraries worldwide. The actual moniker that the white man should go by is not "white supremacist" but "supremacist liar" or instead of "master race" it should be "the master of self-blame."

With all they have done and currently do to Africa, some imbecilic white people have the nerve to claim the entire plight of Africa is caused by their inferior Black genetics. The Democratic Republic of the Congo (DRC) is a classic example of Africans suffering from never ending racism from the aggressor race. They experienced mass looting and a record-breaking genocide at the hands of Belgium's King Leopold followed by decades of Belgium colonization.[111] Unlike France's former colonies controlled solely by France through a colonial tax, today the DRC is neocolonized and controlled by *several outsiders* such as France, Belgium and the United States. In fact the UN and these three countries have military bases inside the DRC.[112]

Sad to say but the DRC will NEVER recover from the Belgium genocide and original colonization. The reason for such universal interest is because the mineral rich Congo has one particular highly prized mineral and that is uranium, the key ingredient needed for atom bombs. For years the UN has occupied the DRC and they are merely proxy operatives acting as white pirates riding around in tanks controlling both the government and the impoverished inhabitants on behalf of white supremacy. When they are not raping women and children the UN regularly steals mineral wealth and smuggles it to neighboring countries for sale.[113]

Under the guise of "peacekeeping" the governors of white power use the UN to consistently rape, spread cholera, steal resources and destabilize mostly Black governments. During so called peacekeeping missions the UN occupiers are almost never prosecuted for sex crimes or any other crime against Black humanity. Ever since Leopold's genocide the Congo has been completely powerless.

Remember, according to idiotic white people the hopelessly deplorable conditions in the DRC have nothing to do with the historical and contemporary facts stated, instead the Africans are plagued by their own corruption and the genetics that causes Black skin. The truth is a violent, lying, sex abusing white scourge has cursed the Congo for being defenseless and possessing a variety of resources including coveted key minerals used for enriching nuclear weapons. Some whites write articles about a so-called "mineral curse" to justify or conceal looting countries into perpetual poverty. The fact is international sponsors of white supremacy is actually that so-called "curse" in living flesh and blood.

If the near powerless Madagascar had oil or uranium the world would witness the same countries exploiting them and placing military bases there. Lucky for Madagascar their top export is vanilla and not gold. Instead of win-win partnerships, white power intends to take all valuables without leaving the Africans as much as a resemblance of ever possessing it. The dire condition of the DRC is due to white power nearly destroying the people and their ongoing control over Congolese affairs. Insecurity rooted in fear of competition, greed, racial hatred, impunity and lust for fighting the defenseless motivates white power to shakedown Africa. Considering the fatal Ebola injections and the deadly inhumane living conditions sponsored by white supremacy, the current white presence in the Congo (and Africa in general) indisputably proves an ongoing extraction and eradication agenda. Genocide can't get any clearer than centuries of killing Africans while presently exterminating them in real time.[114]

Chapter Five:
Responding to Common Racist Talking Points

This bonus chapter discusses moronic people who express the following views. Some don't know any better and deserve an intelligent response to their foolishness.

"Let's face it, the entire world hates Blacks and don't want to be around them."

If that's true it's because the proprietors of white supremacy have been the catalyst for everything that plagues Black people. They have exerted maximum effort to keep Blacks from having wealth and very strong leadership only to highlight the end result of their preventive actions. Blaming Blacks for the end results of detrimental white investment is the trademark of white supremacy.

Those disgraceful final results are sensationalized by white media which keeps the world from scrutinizing the flaws and behavior of the white aggressor race. Step 1, create a range of problems in the Black community. Step 2, blame Black people and connect those problems to Black genetics. Step 3, normalize and increase the pathology created by white power. Step 4, use excessive media coverage to reinforce steps 2 and 3. Step 5, downplay the impetus role white supremacy openly played.

Any group attacked with ongoing extreme racial oppression is bound to be stricken by mental illnesses. The ramifications of centuries of systemic racism include Black people disproportionately suffering from mental health problems. Today many dysfunctional Blacks struggle with depression, anxiety, personality disorders, panic attacks, anger, suicide and other mental disorders only for white society to discharge it as Black genetics acting up again. There are even mental disorders directly connected to slavery and the institutional racism that followed it.[115]

The theory of Post Traumatic Slave Syndrome (PTSS) was developed by Dr. Joy Degruy as a result of twelve years of quantitative and qualitative research. PTSS is rooted in "historical trauma" which currently troubles much of Black America. Dr. Maria Yellow Horse Brave Heart conceptualized "historical trauma" in the 1980s and it is defined as an "example of intergenerational trauma. It's caused by events that target a group of people. Thus, even family members who have not directly experienced the trauma can feel the effects of the event generations later."[116] Historical trauma causes PTSS which is a condition that exists as a consequence of centuries of chattel slavery followed by institutional racism and oppression resulting in multigenerational adaptive behavior, some positive reflecting resilience, and others that are harmful and destructive.[117] PTSS has a range of symptoms including neurotic bouts with anxiety, suspicion, paranoia and could encompass psychotic struggles with violence, rage or abusive behavior. Clinical experts say trauma is embedded into DNA and can alter one's genetic make-up causing the numerous mental and physical health problems that inflict Blacks. If people don't want to be around Blacks it is wholly the fault of white power for creating the kind of impoverished and psychotic Black people easy to hate.[118]

Can you imagine if whites were not on Earth?

To be sure some whites have made great contributions to mankind but based on the real white resume billions of people would celebrate the non-existence of white society. In Australia the Aboriginals use to number three million strong. The white Europeans arrived and promptly started a mass-murderous campaign by shooting, poisoning, stabbing, burning and forcing large numbers of them off cliffs and into the ocean. It was common to bury small children in the sand up to their necks and kick the heads off their bodies and castrate the men in front of their family. When the Europeans were done their genocidal carnage reduced the Aboriginal population from three million to 50,000.

Rape was extremely common both in Australia and in nearby Tasmania, where the most complete genocide in the world was recorded, literally wiping out every last Tasmanian. In America similar genocidal acts occurred culminating in the near complete decimation of the American Indians. Also, for nearly 100 years, in the Deep South white landlords use to collect rent from poor Blacks every Friday and if they didn't have the rent money the landlord would force the Black man to sit on the porch while he raped every female in the home including very young daughters. Very few Black women escaped being raped during slavery and the jim crow era and it was so prevalent that a race of Mulattos was created. Global genocide and rape at the hands of white men is well recorded and those people and their descendants certainly imagine what life would be like if whites weren't on Earth. No white people, no racial slurs for every demographic. No white people, no AIDS or Ebola. No white people, no crack attack. No white people, no nuclear holocaust. No white people, no global genocide.[119]

The view above implies that white people did everything that is noteworthy and the world would collapse without them. Some whites fail to realize that for 363 years American slavery freed up white intellectual property because no one can go out and do what Benjamin Franklin did while also doing what his slaves did such as tending crops and livestock, building barns and homes, clearing trees and building roads, tilling the land and raising his children. According to the real white resume if whites were not on Earth then the Earth itself wouldn't be on its last leg, racism wouldn't be used to rule the world, there wouldn't have been centuries of chattel slavery and no depopulation through vaccines and dangerous lifestyles. The power of diversity guarantees the advanced technology needed to excel would still be intact. White people are roughly 5,000-years-old and white power as we know it is only about 500-years-old, so the world can and has existed without white people.

"We wuz kangs!"

Upon hearing indisputable evidence that Blacks started modern civilization while whites were still primitives living in caves, some whites offer this jealous response rooted in sarcasm. Envy and sarcasm doesn't change the fact that Blacks were attending universities and traveling the world long before anyone white ever put on a shoe.

"Why can't I say nigger? Blacks call each other that."

The dichotomy of the N-Word is rarely discussed. James Braxton Peterson, Director of Africana Studies and associate professor at Lehigh University says "The power of the N-Word comes not only from its historical usage but from Black folk reclaiming the word and trying to divest it of its racialized power and reinvest it with Black vernacular." On the other hand, millions of Blacks are offended by other ignorant blacks who frequently use the word with no regards to their surroundings. Offended Blacks feel other Black people shouldn't habitually use the word and the real question for non-Blacks is, is there any other negative behavior that some black people do that you also want to emulate? Or, when Blacks call each other "brother" do whites wonder out loud if they can also call them brothers? Another consideration should be the poor parenting in the Black community as many parents routinely refer to their children as "lil nigga" as in "shut the damn door lil nigga!" Or, "wake yo' ass up lil nigga!" Many Black children have been called a *lil nigga* by their parent(s) so often it almost replaced their actual name by age five! The Black community has never recovered from centuries of slavery followed by jim crow and persistent racism, only to be completely overwhelmed by a contrived movement to promote the commercial usage of the N-word in order to reinforce the associated characteristics of it with Blacks.

Suit wearing, entertainment controlling white people, rap performers and comedians stopped at nothing to elevate both the word "nigga" and any related negative traits inside the Black community. Their diligent nigga campaigns have successfully convinced many Black people to substantially live up to the moniker and embrace the associated behavior as "Black behavior." Today Black people raise their children on violent self-defiling rap, beginning in the hospital parking lot when they first place their newborn into a car playing violent rap music. Heavily sponsoring the N-word is another example of white supremacists executing a villainous plan and then blaming Blacks for the negative end results of that plan. "You call each other nigger all the time!" Response, "In order to divide Blacks and keep them as child-like as possible, white power relentlessly invested billions of dollars saturating the community with "nigga" to normalize and deeply ingrain it into the Black community!" [120]

"Why are you angry about police killing Blacks with so much black-on-black crime?"

People are right to suggest that the Black community should have a stronger response to blacks killing Blacks. But police murdering unarmed Blacks and black-on-black crime is two different problems. The blacks who kill other Blacks are oftentimes gangsters who are usually arrested and imprisoned for their crimes; as public servants the police swore to uphold the constitution and are professional government officials paid by taxpayers who rarely get arrested for murdering Blacks. Another consideration is that blacks have been excessively killing Blacks since the 1980s (after crack and machine guns was introduced) or over 40 years, but law enforcement has been routinely killing unarmed Blacks for hundreds of years.

When Blacks complain about police brutality they are reminded of black-on-black crime, but if they complain about black-on-black crime they would not be advised to address police brutality. People bring up "black-on-black crime" during discussions of killer-cops, but they don't bring up "killer-cops" during the discussion of black-on-black crime. If the two issues are intertwined and people are going to bring up black-on-black crime whenever cops brutalize Black people, why don't they do the reverse and bring up killer-cops when discussing black-on-black crime? The answer is because they know the two problems are unrelated. Furthermore, homicidal blacks are influenced by the drugs and alcohol that white power puts into Black areas, they are using the guns that the government has provided and white America insists that citizens have, they are full of self-hatred that white society has taught them, they are fatherless gang members influenced by the kind of rap music that white society controls and wants them to hear.[121] Black youth were not frequently killing each other when they had fathers, the Black Panthers and strong Black leadership, something white power destroyed. They are also killing people who they usually have a beef with, unlike the white mass shooters killing total strangers. Whites kill other whites and that doesn't justify police killing unarmed white citizens, and when a black person kills another it doesn't give a license for everyone else to kill Blacks. It's amazing how simpletons are so unaware of such rudimentary facts.

White society has a lot to do with black-on-black violence. Let's take the "model minority" Asians. Repeat the following steps and see what the end result would be: (1) Destroy and replace their vital leadership with gang members and demolish their cohesive organizations. (2) Disintegrate their families by removing Asian fathers through lengthy prison sentences and aggressive child support and replace them with gangster rappers and homosexuals. (3) Saturate their areas with crack and follow that with malt liquor and machine guns. (4) Pay their youth to popularize gang and criminal activity through songs. (5) Invest heavily in their self-hatred. (6) Expose them to a criminally inferior education. (7) Subject them to urban renewal and "last hired, first fired." (8) Frequently televise the resulting pathologies. (9) Keep them poor. (10) Allow those pathologies to spiral out of control and what would you have? You'd have Asian-on-Asian crime identical to black-on-black crime. If a Black leader successfully lowered black violence white power would audit his taxes and threaten his life.[122]

Many Blacks reject the gun culture, did not import metric tons of crack, desire to have a nuclear family, would change or cancel violent rap music, and crave for leaders like Martin Luther King and Malcolm X, everything opposite to what white power has in store for Black America.

"The data proves whites are superior and Blacks are inferior."

We rarely hear Blacks boast about being superior to whites in anything they have proven to be dominant in, and many arenas that Blacks currently dominate white people previously dominated. Being superior means not needing to cheat and undermine others to prevent them from having wealth, leadership or weapons systems comparable to yours. Superiority is not denying others equal opportunity in order to be superior or even worrying about competition. For example, every average grown man is superior to all five-year-olds when it comes to arm wrestling. Not a single man needs to cheat and in fact their superiority is so absolute that they can give a head-start or other advantages and still win at arm wrestling. That example shows the difference between actual superiority and a group claiming superiority but doing everything possible to inhibit fair competition.

Rendering and keeping others defenseless or incapable of challenging is a distinctive emblem of white supremacy. White supremacists clamor for a race war with a vulnerable Black minority who can't effectively fight back. Militarily, white power only fights others who can't truly fight back, allowing white power to look superior. Nonbelievers can check the list of countries the U.S. or Russia has gone to war with and try counting other superpowers. You'll find lots of wars and zero superpower opponents going all the way back to Hitler and WWII—and Hitler was a solid underdog who couldn't strike the United States. Any country with the ability to project war and consistently bomb white power is safe from military confrontation.

In schools across America, statistics don't lie; Blacks are genetically inferior to whites.

This claim is rooted in eugenics or bogus scientific conclusions claiming that the color white is superior to Black, both genetically and by default. Academically this myth was debunked long ago but that has never stopped others from claiming it is a fact and pointing to academic statistics for proof. Even though Black African immigrants are the most educated in the U.S., this racist lie continues to exist.[123] The truth is there are too many outstanding Black individuals who have surpassed everyone else including other outstanding students. That fact negates the false inferiority claim because if a group was genetically inferior it would be impossible to find a single exception. In science it only takes a solitary exception to prove a theory wrong.

In 2020, a Miami teenager named Temi Adelakun made history by becoming the first Black valedictorian at South Broward High School. With a grade point average of 5.6214 Temi set another record by graduating with the highest GPA ever recorded at his school. In 2019 Elijah Precciely became the youngest person in history to receive a full scholarship to Southern University. His classmates described this 11-year-old physics major as one of the smartest people on campus. In 2019, a homeless teen named Tupac Mosley made the news for becoming high school valedictorian. He received three million dollars in scholarships and offers from 40 universities. In college Tupac majored in engineering. In 2018, Darrel Kelly graduated from two different universities on the same day with two advanced degrees. Darrel graduated from high school at 16-years-old and then graduated from Howard University four years later with a degree in radio, television and film. From there he went on to get a law degree from the University Of Cincinnati College Of Law and a Master of Business Administration from Xavier University. At 24-years-old Kelly got two advanced degrees from two different universities on the same day. Some studies suggest Black women are among the most educated demographics in the U.S.[124] At 13-years-old Kimora Hudson was the youngest student to be accepted and taking classes at The University of West Georgia. Caleb Anderson started reading at six-months-old, learned sign language at nine-months-old, was doing fractions at two and enrolled at Chattahoochee Technical College in Marietta by age 12.

White society has never highly valued the intellectual capital within the Black community, especially Black men. In fact for hundreds of years they prohibited Blacks from reading and writing because ignorance was used to control African slaves. For centuries intelligence was an undesirable trait in Blacks and to this day much of white society remains fearful of astute Black men. Instead of pursuing Black academic excellence many white controlled institutions heavily invest in establishing and monetizing marketable pathologies like gang activity and hyper-sex instead of cultivating educational high achievers.

For example, one strategy to undermine Blacks in education is to offer billions of dollars to young blacks to perform violent rap music or participate in sports. Once they aspire to excel in rap music or sports Black students lowered their value for education. Some even say out loud "learning and school is for white people." By paying unrealistic dollars to uneducated youth to promote criminality white society steered them away from education and towards delinquency and entertainment. Countless kids not yet 13-years-old are already polished rappers who spend most nights rehearsing appalling rap lyrics instead of doing homework. The mind boggling money and incredible fame proves irresistible and a pipeline away from higher education is established.

White society heavily rewards blacks for performing negative rap music or cross-dressing more than they reward Black professionals. A black sell-out who strongly supports gay rights or raps about shooting Black citizens can earn more than four Black engineers put together. Countless popular rappers were active criminals and drive-by shooters while offered million-dollar contracts by white power. Ask yourself, how does someone commit homicide in a gang related drive-by shooting, bail out and then immediately sign a contract for millions of dollars? Where are the white gang members receiving the same million-dollar paydays for killing other whites?

Some claim Blacks have a lower IQ but instead of mining for Black academic excellence white individuals are the ones stupid enough to pay hundreds of millions of dollars annually to gangsters to promote criminal pathology. That is a dumb low-IQ investment because while it fulfills the goal of killing off Black citizens the fact is every society is only as strong as their weakest link. Instead of investing in Black doctors, engineers, lawyers, construction workers and patriotism apparently white society prefers to see pestilence which causes others to question the IQ status of some white people.

"Just admit it, Blacks have low IQ."

Okay, regrettably, sometimes it is true. When Blacks worship a fake white Jesus they demonstrate low spiritual IQ. When Blacks patronize racist businesses they exhibit low economic IQ. When Blacks vote for political parties that ignore their needs they illustrate low political IQ. When Black Americans are featured happy and smiling in HIV medicine commercials or demonstrate for risky lifestyles rife with AIDS they showcase low wellness IQ. When Africans allow millions of Chinese to flood and populate their countries while openly hating Black skin and African people then their sanity as well as IQ must be considered.

Actually "IQ" isn't the only measurement for intelligence and what composes intelligence are the 3 Q's; the Intelligent Quotient (**IQ**), the Emotional Quotient (**EQ**) and the Spiritual Quotient (**SQ**) are equal in importance.[125]

"If Blacks and Latinos outnumber whites in the U.S. the country will become a third world nation. They should go back to where they came from."

If they went "back to where they came from" you would travel there and torment them the same way you do in the U.S. Whites didn't develop the U.S. alone and if the innovations and efforts of Blacks and Latinos were removed the U.S. would be an undeveloped country. If Blacks and Latinos actually left the U.S. and took all of their assets with them the U.S. would go from developed to struggling. There are an estimated 1.1 million doctors in the United States with approximately six percent of them Black and about six percent Latino. While that percentage is low numerically those figures come out to over 65,000 Black and 65,000 Latino doctors.

The U.S. needs over 40,000 doctors to meet current needs and can't afford to lose 130,000 doctors. Blacks and Latinos have been in every war the U.S. has ever had and white people who like to tell others to "go back" do so while standing as far away from Iceland as possible. Many white ethnics have only been in the U.S. for less than 250 years and therefore are telling others who were there first to leave—talk about white privilege and entitlement. Even President Trump admitted that Blacks built the country.[126]

"Blacks have an entitlement mentality."

For some strange reason the entitlement mentality discussion is limited to welfare and social security. What about white entitlement mentality? They feel entitled to put their white face on Jesus, destroy the Earth, tell natives to leave their own country, possess thousands of atom bombs while preventing sovereign nations from having just one, regulate fertility rates for other groups, and name laws, holidays and systems like the Amber Alert after themselves. Some white governed countries feel entitled to steal artifacts and place them in museums for profit. Slave owners were entitled to compensation when slavery ended but white governments and corporations refuse to pay a dime to their former slaves or their descendants. Some whites feel entitled to protest a Farrakhan speech on a platform aimed at a Black audience. Many whites think they personally own everything and feel entitled to authoritatively question someone moving into "their" apartment building or riding a bicycle down "their" street. Others feel entitled to harass people with racial slurs or control Black leadership and organizations, networks and businesses; white folks are the last people who should be pointing out an entitlement mentality or engaging in the discussion.

"Blacks are the most violent people on Earth; Chicago is more violent than Afghanistan."

Sad to say but at first glance it does appear that Blacks are the most violent people but that violence is primarily street behavior and gang violence. Violence is not only measured by street activity but also includes other worldly sectors and white society is more violent in virtually all other categories. White power has traveled the world committing the most genocide; a white controlled government and military has the distinction of using atom bombs; white Americans insist on having a gun culture; white businessmen use violence as a cornerstone in movies, video games and music. A white dominated U.S. Government maintains a permanent war due to the 9/11 attack that happened over 20 years ago, and has killed over 2 million innocent civilians in response to the death of 3000 U.S. citizens in the 9/11 attacks. Furthermore, whites are usually the perpetrators who commit annual mass shootings against total strangers.

While blacks are the most violent people in the streets whites also have violent street gangs, and that excludes monstrous vigilantes and brutal police. The claim that blacks are the most violent people is another attempt to deflect attention away from themselves and onto Blacks. Some whites are notorious for accusing Blacks of something that actually applies to them. "Blacks steal so much" when whites have stolen history, religion, mineral wealth, resources, labor, thousands of artifacts and land all over the world—which excludes other forms of grand theft like patent trolling, ransomware and ponzi schemes. "Blacks do a lot of drugs" when whites do more and a wider variety. "Blacks are lazy" when whites enjoyed centuries of free labor and still use slavery today. "Blacks are perverted" when whites normalized HIV by showcasing happy HIV+ people in televised HIV medicine commercials. "Black Lives Matter is a terrorist organization" when confederates and the KKK have a track record of life-threatening terrorism. "Blacks are more racist than whites" when every housing, employment and civil rights law written is because of white racism. "Blacks are rapists" when white men have raped so much internationally that another demographic now exists. "Blacks are spear-chuckers" when mostly whites win Olympic gold medals for throwing the javelin. "Blacks are unintelligent" when whites inject Blacks with drugs that cause autism and provide lead-poisoned water to expedite learning disabilities. "Blacks originated drive-by shootings" when white cowboys were doing ride-by shootings and indiscriminately shooting up towns on horseback hundreds of years ago. "Blacks don't want to work" when whites put job resumes with "Black sounding names" into the trashcan. "Blacks are hyper-sexed" when whites establish international sex tourism and control a trillion dollar sex toy and porn industry. "Blacks should get over slavery" when whites vehemently defend every aspect of the confederacy. "Whites are being replaced" when it is whites systematically committing global genocide.

When it comes to the violence in cities like Chicago there are questions that need to be asked and the answers reflects the role white power plays in that violence. Who insists that the U.S. has a gun culture? White people. Who killed and co-opted influential Black leadership and organizations that would have challenged criminal behavior? White people. Who overwhelmed Blacks with the crack and malt liquor often associated with Black violence? White people. Who sponsors self-destructive gang violence through rap music? White people. Who falsified African history and taught Blacks the self-hatred intricate to black-on-black crime? White people. Who controls most economic opportunities? White people. Who controls a powerful police force, herculean government, policies and media capable of wiping out black gangs inside three years? White people.

To resolve the dilemma white power must partner with the Black community and (1) stop acting like black gangs are so invincible they can't be stopped, (2) help restore the traditional family, (3) remove the drugs and curtail guns, (4) discontinue the self-sabotaging rap music, (5) increase opportunities, (6) allow strong Black leadership independent of white control, (7) stop teaching self-hatred by withholding Black history and those changes will transform Black America, consequently causing black crime and violence to plummet. *Any three of these ideas would noticeably lower black-on-black crime.* This is another example of white society blaming others for the end results of their own actions and inactions.[g]

---

[g] Destroying neighborhoods with freeways directly contributes to crime, Chicago Department of Urban Renewal Records,

"Blacks were happy slaves, we did them a favor."

That use to be a common sentiment until historians produced evidence of over 220 *recorded* slave revolts, not counting hundreds of unrecorded insurrections. Some still claim slavery was a blessing for Blacks and they like to show images of African mud-huts while doing so. But if Africa is so awful why can't the Africans get 10 million Chinese and hundreds of millions of white people to leave Africa? That statement is based mostly on economics but millions of Africans live better than millions of whites in the U.S. and Europe. Finally, hate-filled white people coldheartedly enslaved American Blacks for 363 years, since when do hateful people do favors for those they hate?

"Look at Asian countries; they are prosperous and not complaining about past racism."

Comparing Asians and Blacks is usually done by white supremacists and rarely done by Asians. What is even rarer is for these comparisons to be based on performance that highlights Black excellence, such developing musical genres or securing the most patents between 1865 and 1965, Out of dozens of Asian countries, only four are considered fully industrialized and they are Japan, Singapore, South Korea and Taiwan. "Conservatives" haven't murdered dozens of Asian leaders or overthrown governments, executed charity schemes, forced roaming wildlife to remain, imposed economic sanctions over frivolous reasons or implemented neocolonialism. White power takes it easy on Asia. Britain took Hong Kong from China and developed it into a beautiful country. When they returned it they didn't impose ongoing debilitating colonial taxes that white power levied on Haiti and West Africa, who experienced a fraction of Hong Kong's development.[127]

---

https://www.chipublib.org/fa-chicago-department-of-urban-renewal-records/

Look at the global pass given to China. If any African country allowed Covid-19 to leave its border and devastate economies and infect the world including world leaders that country would face either trillion dollar lawsuits or be toppled. If any African nation stole as much top-secret intellectual property as China has that country's government would be heavily sanctioned or overthrown. Japan was conquered with nuclear weapons but instead of subjugating them for exploitation white power partnered with the Japanese and even gave them honorary white status. Apparently the fear and insecurity that accommodates Black competitiveness isn't manifested and extended to Asian competitiveness. In fact white supremacy has invested trillions of dollars into developing all the "light-skinned" Asian nations listed. Black people have been overcome and disenfranchised by a terrified enemy too worried about being conquered themselves to equally partner with Black people.[128]

"We are being replaced, a white genocide is happening."

No outside demographic forced abortion, crack-cocaine and alternative lifestyles on you. Toxic dumpsites aren't routinely placed near predominately white areas.[129] Nobody invented a disease like AIDS to kill you off. No one lead-poisoned your water or stuck you with needles full of mystery vaccines designed to cause infertility, autism and early death. No one is inside hospitals unplugging machines or using lethal injections as you critically suffer from Covid-19.[130] Few whites are dying from the death penalty; there is no mass incarceration program targeting you; racist systems don't cripple you with poverty or deny you adequate health care; nobody is encouraging white youth to commit fratricide by targeting them with self-hating music; if whites are rapidly dying off they are contributing to their own demise.[h]

"All lives matter!"

Not until Black lives matter too. If white power can do everything listed in this book without paying fair reparations for a 450 year Black Holocaust then Black lives doesn't matter.

Look at African migrants risking their lives to be around white people! Why are they always trying to live around white people?

It's amazing that Africans can't get white people out of Africa no matter what, yet some people make this comment. Also, Europe and America plundered Africa and still do. It's human nature to desire close proximity to stolen resources in order to benefit from those resources. Africans see the national flags on the ships and planes that carry off their mineral wealth and they follow suit. That appears to be the best way to benefit from ill-begotten resources.

"Trump was right; Africa is full of shithole countries."

Lack of infrastructure is not the only way to define a "shithole" country. A country that has a violent gun culture and senseless mass shootings, hateful militias, routine gang violence, rampant same-sex activity, crack-cocaine and opioid addiction, readily available pornography accessible to young children, a stripper culture, miserable traffic jams, abusive police and systemic racism can easily be defined as a shithole country too.

---

[h] *White-on-white murder in America is out of control,* Matthew Yglesias, February 20, 2015, *Vox*, https://www.vox.com/2014/8/21/6053811/white-on-white-murder

"There's no racism, it's your imagination or leftist lies."

Fair enough—gold is worthless, one plus one is five, water is not wet, the surface of the sun is cold, Blue whales are tiny…This silly racist opinion should not even be debated.

"Black Lives Matter is a terrorist organization!"

The founders and members of Black Lives Matter don't have a large cache of weapons or stockpiles of ammunition. This demonizing name-calling strategy is not new; racists have historically reclassified any effort to obtain justice. Dr. King fought for basic rights like voting and eating inside a restaurant and for that he was called "communist." The next generation of freedom fighters sought fair housing and employment and that earned them the title "radicals" and "extremists." Today equality activists are seeking law enforcement accountability so their enemies find it suitable to call them "thugs" and "terrorists." Same tactic, different description.[i]

---

[i] *White Supremacists Are Top Terror Threat In DHS Draft Assessments: Report,* Mary Papenfuss, September 5, 2020, *HuffPost,*

https://www.yahoo.com/huffpost/white-supremacists-biggest-terror-threat-dhs-130451980.html

Conclusion

"We charge genocide: The Crime of Government against the Negro People." That was the title of a petition written in 1951 by the Civil Rights Congress (CRC) and presented to the United Nations. The document itemized the treatment of Black Americans and pointed out that the U.S. treatment of Blacks easily met the definition of genocide provided by the UN. The authors honed in on Article C of the charter that defines genocide in part as "any acts committed with the intent to destroy in whole or in part" another group.[131]

The CRC based their case on thousands of lynchings, systemic racism, police brutality, countless cases of wrongful capital punishment, voter suppression, poverty and the lack of health care and legal discrimination. The 237-page petition included that:

"The oppressed Negro citizens of the United States, segregated, discriminated against, and long the target of violence, suffer from genocide as the result of the consistent, conscious, unified policies of every branch of government. If the General Assembly acts as the conscience of mankind and therefore acts favorably on our petition, it will have served the cause of peace."

The CRC asserted that the U.S. Government endorsed genocide through racism and "monopoly capitalism," stating, "The persistent, constant, widespread, institutionalized commission of the crime of genocide would be impossible." Stressing the urgency, they emphasized that the genocide was fueled by white supremacy and drew parallels between the American and Nazi genocides. The document emphasized post-1945 incidents and presented a compelling case, acknowledged even by some opponents for its factual accuracy. The U.S. media largely ignored the petition or dismissed it as "shameful lies." The government downplayed racism, accused the petition of exaggeration, and harassed its proponents. Following CRC Secretary William Patterson's presentation of the petition to the UN in Paris, the U.S. State Department retaliated by compelling him to surrender his passport. To avoid collateral damage, the government enlisted Raphael Lemkin, who coined the term "genocide," to discredit the document. He accused its authors, Patterson and Robeson, of attempting to divert attention from the alleged genocide in the Soviet Union. Lemkin claimed they were working for foreign governments, given their communist sympathies.

In a New York Times op-ed, Lemkin argued that Black Americans did not undergo the "destruction, death, and annihilation" that would categorize their treatment as genocide. This highlights how many only acknowledge genocide when it occurs rapidly and violently, overlooking the slower, systematic methods that diminish fertility rates. Genocide, as per the UN definition, involves not just aggressive mass killing but also the significant and systematic reduction of a group's population.

While the petition received little attention in the U.S., it garnered widespread support globally, particularly in South East Asia, Africa, and Europe. However, due to its communist backing, the U.S. Government dismantled the CRC in 1956 during the Red Scare. As a major UN contributor, the U.S. urged the organization to claim they never received the petition, effectively ending its impact. Nonetheless, the petition's legacy endured, inspiring other Black activists to carry on the cause. The Black Panthers, Malcolm X, and other Black organizations, along with the literary community, popularized the term "Black Genocide" within the community. Allegations of genocide resurfaced after government actions involving crack-cocaine and HIV. In 1996-1997, the National Black United Front re-petitioned the United Nations, referencing "We Charge Genocide" and adopting the same slogan. Their petition begins with the following statements:

> Declaration of Genocide by the U.S. Government Against the Black Population in the United States.

> Whereas, we the undersigned people of African ancestry understand that the proliferation of the distribution and sale of crack cocaine...has reached epidemic proportions, causing serious harm to the African community in the United States. Therefore, we understand that this harm can only be described as acts of genocide by the United States government through its Central Intelligence Agency.
>
> In addition to acts of genocide perpetuated through the CIA and in this recent revelation, acts of genocide can also be attributed to the Government's use of taxpayers' resources to wage war on a segment of the U.S. population. This is evidenced by the following: (1) cutting back on welfare; (2) privatization of public housing and land grab schemes; (3) privatization of public education; (4) racist immigration policies; (5) privatization of basic health care; (6) building prisons and the expanding incarceration of millions of African and Latino youth.[132]

Today, the situation remains unchanged, except for the introduction of lethal weapons detailed in this book. These weapons have claimed millions of Black lives and inflicted economic devastation, reducing the potential population by an estimated 70 to 90% within 50 years. Abortion, coupled with the effects of incarceration and birth-control initiatives, constitutes a holocaustic trifecta responsible for the death of over 20 million Black babies. The abortion of 20 million Black babies alone represents a staggering 50% of the current Black American population. Black lives are systematically diminished both at the beginning and end of life – reduced through birth control, abortions, and high infant mortality, and later impacted by diseases, perilous lifestyles, violence, poverty, and incarceration—constituting genocide.

Opponents of Black Genocide argue that the Black American population is growing, undermining any genocide claims. However, compared to other racial groups with healthier birthrates, Black Americans exhibit a mere 0.5% growth rate over 20 years, an anomaly.

In 2000, Blacks were 12.9%, in 2010, 13.6%, and in 2020, 13.4% of the U.S. population. (Latinos increased from 12.5% in 2000 to 18.5% in 2020) White supremacy proponents strategically control the Black birthrate, meeting several genocide criteria.

Despite ample evidence, some deny the claims in this book, asserting, "All issues in Black America are self-inflicted," and "AIDS wasn't created as a bioweapon," and "Crack wasn't introduced into the Black community," and "Assassinations of your leaders don't matter," and "The Black community wasn't targeted with guns, abortion, or risky lifestyles. Throughout this book, it is emphasized that white power introduces pathologies into the Black community, then attributes them to Black genetics or culture to conceal the white origins of those pathologies. Designated public enemy number one without cause, Black men and women confront attacks from both political directions, experiencing subtle and overt aggression. Leftist white power deploys leadership control, abortion, and alternative lifestyles as principal weapons, utilizing politics, censorship, and open targeting to suppress Black fertility rates. The far-right resorts to denial, self-blame, violent vigilantes, and biased law enforcement for mass incarceration, while the far-left deploys incentives like bribery and Hollywood acceptance to promote specific agendas through sensational entertainers, endorsing institutional racism. The far-right subtly communicates with extremists, fosters fear of integration, and denies white privilege and systemic racism to impede meaningful dialogue. Both sides dismiss valid criticism, uphold white dominance, and lack genuine support for Black liberation. In the words of John Henrik Clarke, "Blacks don't have any friends."[133]

With minimal support and the marginal growth of a vulnerable Black America, the future raises concerns. *Black American History* unequivocally reveals an unbalanced, three-dimensional racist war against Black society. The weapons of control and genocide encompass Uncle Toms, neglect, vigilante violence, substances like crack and alcohol, AIDS, legal systems, urban renewal, birth control, alternative lifestyles, abortion, infant mortality, prison, vaccinations, politics, media, law enforcement, propaganda, government actions, and inactions. These all-inclusive, targeted tactics encompass every facet of Black life, affecting health, sexuality, finances, freedom, mental well-being, and most significantly, BIRTHRATE.

These lethal strategies extend to a range of subsidiary tactics aiming to eradicate Black individuals, encompassing fast-food, contaminated water, denial, stress, self-hatred, discriminatory lending practices, normalized gun violence, hazardous waste sites, refineries, and gentrification leading to poverty and homelessness. Their primary and secondary tier of racial warfare operations are diverse, covering legal, economic, chemical, biological, and depopulation aspects. The multitude of weapons results in a spectrum of fatal outcomes, ranging from severe devastation to outright liquidation. These stark realities underscore an ongoing, one-sided, race-driven war, highlighting the profound physiological and psychological impact of white supremacy on its victims.

Historically, mental illnesses play a role in facilitating extermination, as societal conditioning is necessary for a holocaust to be accepted. Currently, Black individuals encounter peculiar reactions during routine activities. Many whites are mentally averse to seeing Blacks, exhausted by the "niggers" they created, and are eager for an immediate elimination. This clarifies why someone could be reported to homicidal police for simply drinking a cup of coffee. The excess vitriol stems from centuries of accumulated insecurity, hatred, and media portrayals. With the groundwork for genocide in place, white society is now eager for the extermination process.

What does it signify when the broader society openly detests encountering you in any situation? It indicates that beneath the surface lies an immense amount of fear and resentment, which will eventually reach a boiling point. No other community would tolerate the abusive treatment detailed in this book, and still desire to reside or interact with such a racially motivated, psychopathic, and relentless aggressor. Traumatized and unaware, Black individuals are overlooking the gravity of the historical racial torment, leading them to misunderstand the ongoing holocaust. Black people need to be globally informed, plainly: "For many, the life of a solitary 9-year-old white girl is deemed more valuable than the lives of all Black Americans combined; many white individuals harbor more hatred than you realize, and they have normalized genocide. Wake up or face extinction."

Under-reporting various white extermination methods lead to unawareness and a subdued response to the systematic killing of Black people. For instance, few Black individuals are aware that in 1939, the abortion industry was named The Negro Project, openly centered on Black population control, specifically designed to diminish the Black American population. "We do not want word to go out that we want to exterminate the Negro population," Sanger wrote —*Letter to Dr. Clarence Gamble on Dec., 10, 1939.* Black Americans also fail to realize they have been 13% of the population for over 25 years.

Over time, gradual ethnic cleansing numbs and anesthetizes the targeted population, aiding Blacks in adapting to state-sponsored death and leading to a long-term "normalized systematic genocide." However, initiating a prolonged race war has a different impact on white society. Over time, white people recognize that a group enduring three-dimensional and relentless state-sponsored racism-related murder is genuinely strong and resilient.

If given an equitable opportunity, this demographic could contend for power. White society concludes that the unorganized, misguided, and leaderless Black population has withstood generational, multi-genocidal efforts, survived, somewhat prospered, and is poised to return to past glory if not racially undermined. There is a fear in white society that an advanced Black society may retaliate and reciprocate the treatment received by Black people.

Combining ingrained white societal hatred and phobia with their fear of potential retaliation and the emergence of a fully developed Black race, it is evident that their deepest fear is being conquered. Given that white people are not inherently racially superior, systemic racism becomes their primary tool to thwart the threatening development and potential conquest by Black society.

When you factor in the direct and subliminal anti-Black messages perpetuated by the media, the resulting terror is so extreme that frightened white individuals experience hallucinations and nightmares. These compounded elements lead to irrational and inexplicable psychotic overreactions in their actual interactions with Black people.

For example, an innocent Black man gets shot while jogging; numerous small school children are handcuffed and arrested over tantrums; ten heavily-armed white authoritarian police openly fear diminutive, non-aggressive, unarmed Black men and women—resulting in six patrol cars responding to a petty charge like jaywalking; horrified middle-income white homeowners don't want *affluent* Blacks to move next door; terrified white politicians openly and illegally suppress miniscule "minority" Black votes out of fear of a "large" turnout and jittery well-trained police *regularly* "fear for their lives" and confuse mobile phones and car-keys with firearms. When it comes to dealing with scary-ass white folks the one thing Black folks should fear more than anything else is how incredibly preoccupied they are with Black people.

Writing this book required studying genocide worldwide, including Hitler. In nearly every instance of genocide there has been a conditioning of the minds and hearts of both the larger society and the victims of genocide. When discussing how Hitler used propaganda to condition society and white Jews for genocide here is what the United States Holocaust Memorial Museum stated:

> Following the Nazi seizure of power in 1933, Hitler established a Reich Ministry of Public Enlightenment and Propaganda headed by

> Joseph Goebbels. The Ministry's aim was to ensure that the Nazi message was successfully communicated through art, music, theater, films, books, radio, educational materials, and the press.
>
> There were several audiences for Nazi propaganda. Germans were reminded of the struggle against foreign enemies and Jewish subversion. During periods preceding legislation or executive measures against Jews, propaganda campaigns created an atmosphere tolerant of violence against Jews, particularly in 1935 (before the Nuremberg Race Laws of September) and in 1938…Propaganda also encouraged passivity and acceptance of the impending measures against Jews, as these appeared to depict the Nazi government as stepping in and "restoring order."[134]

People should be alarmed that the same propaganda and techniques are in effect today. If Black Americans could not achieve much when they were the second-largest population and currently struggle as the third-largest group, it is highly unlikely they will accomplish anything significant as one of the smallest demographics. Time is not on Black America's side.

This chapter focuses on the term "pragmatic," defined as dealing sensibly and realistically with practical rather than theoretical reasons. By pragmatically examining how life operates, several fair conclusions about the intentions of white supremacy emerge. Analogously, if someone gifts another person an expensive home gym, it is fair to conclude the buyer wants them to embrace fitness. Similarly, if a person provides another with a guard dog and a firearm, it is evident that the buyer prefers them to have personal protection.

Applying pragmatism makes it clear what the enforcers of white power seek for Black society. If a dominant group inundates a selected community with substantial amounts of crack-cocaine and inexpensive malt liquor, they aim for chemical dependency. When thousands of police can fatally shoot unarmed Blacks numerous times for trivial or no reasons without facing accountability, it reveals a lack of concern for Black lives.

If an entity promotes HIV medicine with cheerful Black men kissing and embracing their HIV positive status in commercials, the evident goal is for Blacks to contract the disease. If a dominant group systematically directs a smaller group toward abortions or a prison pipeline, it unmistakably indicates a desire to reduce the birthrate of that group. Genocidal actions occur when a larger population dismantles the traditional family structure in a smaller demographic and subsequently inundates them with dangerous behavior linked to deadly diseases. When white power prohibited the effective use of DDT and hindered Africa from eradicating malaria, it evidently signaled an eagerness to witness countless Africans succumb to malaria.[135] All the points made so far are pragmatic. Black individuals should cease expecting confessions from creatively ingenious racist adversaries, and draw their own conclusions based on practical results derived from adverse actions committed by members of the white community.

The most glaring feature of the white community's murderous history is its unapologetic stance towards centuries of holocaustic treatment. Seldom have they expressed remorse for extensive sinister mistreatment, revealing the true sentiments of many white individuals towards Blacks. To date, there has been no meaningful apology to Africans or the Diaspora for over 300 years of slavery or 100 years of colonization, no contrition for a century of Jim Crow, no repentance for systematically extending slavery another 100 years through strategies like prison labor and sharecropping, no remorse for using chemical and biological agents (crack, AIDS) against Blacks, no sorrow for shamelessly targeting Black society for same-sex birth control schemes, and no regrets for stealing history. Additionally, there is fierce opposition to reparations for 500 years of blatant, multi-level, structural disparities and crimes committed against Black humanity.

This book exposes white society's systematic weapons for controlling and annihilating Black communities. Phrases like "Get over it," and "nobody owes Black people anything," and "Blacks deserve it" appear to align with a default white perspective. Alternatively, recognizing that white people, society, and power bear significant responsibility for the challenges facing Black communities is crucial. Acknowledging this one-sided war is the first step in addressing the systemic attack and removal, dispelling the notion that appalling statistics result from inherent Black traits. These disturbing statistics are a product of racist attitudes among insecure white individuals, not divine curses or genetic predispositions. If white society ever wants to admire their genocidal handy work they can just categorically review the data associated with Black society.

Recognizing targeted depopulation necessitates developing defenses against race-based attacks. Essential measures include promoting nuclear families with strong fatherhood, fostering group economics, empowering nationally recognized leaders for critical responses, establishing self-funded organizations dedicated to group survival, and upholding basic moral values rooted in faith. The Black elite and business class must take the lead in creating nationwide independent commercial financial districts, based on vertically controlled business structures, to facilitate upward mobility. Without these defenses, a vulnerable group remains easily manipulated by the larger society. Drowning in alternative lifestyles, drugs, crime, poverty, and disease, current Black statistics mirror the goals of white supremacy, with none of the mentioned defenses showing any signs of embryonic development.

Apart from increasing awareness, the pivotal change needed is to resist media influence and firmly reject financially incentivized individuals who contribute to molding Blacks into whatever suits white society's desires. These payouts assist white power in transforming Blacks into entities devoid of respect, fair compensation, or ties to historical greatness. Currently whatever white people want for Blacks can be achieved through bribing blacks and persistent advertisements. Presently if they yearn to grow alternative lifestyles or popularize ghetto behavior, no problem; simply showcase blacks as such and subsidize celebrities to sponsor the message. If they aim to promote alcoholism or obesity, it is achieved effortlessly—simply showcase compensated Black actors repeatedly drinking or consuming unhealthy food. To escalate gang activity, produce and circulate violent movies or music, and compensate Black individuals to endorse the product. Consider this: several Black American billionaires have participated in or sponsored detrimental behavior to amass billions. Dr. Dre and Jay-Z endorsed drug dealing and violence. Oprah Winfrey consistently promoted dangerous lifestyles during the AIDS epidemic. Tyler Perry portrayed emasculated Black men. Kanye West embraced gratuitous vulgarity, and Michael Jordan largely overlooked racism.

Emphatically, the Black community must reject inducements and denounce hostile media that consistently commercializes pathology and devalues Black life. White forces heavily invest in portraying Blacks as ignorant, criminal, and impoverished. When they reap the dividends of this investment, they attribute it to Black genetics, showcasing their distorted image of Black society for global condemnation. Blacks must discern psychological manipulation and disown any recurrent targeted marketing aimed at indoctrinating Black America into a sick and eventually non-existent society. Uniquely for Blacks, no other group witnesses their criminal class amassing wealth; it literally pays to embrace juvenile, violent, and gangster behavior when it comes to blacks and white supremacy. Group survival hinges on condemning financially rewarded misbehavior, and recognizing harmful disinformation directed towards Black Genocide.

Black American History has diligently exposed the genocidal tools at play, and underscored the influence wielded by the guardians of white power on Black societies. However, the book remains incomplete without offering vital strategies for survival. *The American Directory of Certified Uncle Toms* offers valuable counsel on thwarting complete eradication:

> Any self-respecting, independent people made aware of this [genocidal] threat to its group survival *immediately* organizes resources to correct the maladies. Leaders sound the alarm and establish the national dialogue and an action agenda; the media broadcast the threat and the urgency of an immediate response; educational institutions and their scholars refocus to confront the crisis and compose enlightened solutions; defensive forces are dispatched to expel malignant external encroachment; emergency relief is organized for those most in need; the legal system is mobilized to punish the aggressors and to legislate for future abatement of threat; and the national agenda is altered accordingly to circumvent or prevent any future occurrence...Such was the response for the attacks on the US on September 11, 2001which killed 3000 innocent civilians. But no such response for massacring millions of people in the Black Holocaust.

On page 43 the team of professionals continues:

> If a Black man or woman, when faced with this clear evidence of genocide *refuses* to take responsibility in some tangible form to defend the race and remedy the existing condition, or denies the validity of the complaint, or blames the victims of white supremacy, that Black man or woman will be subject to some form of chastisement by the practicing members of the Black race.[136]

Exploring historical structural persecution can deeply affect a researcher, personally and even spiritually. For those who believe in God and delve into the study of racism, pragmatic questions may arise. When it becomes evident that white society has acted with impunity, these questions are voiced aloud.

What kind of God allows the white man to destroy the planet? What kind of God allows white society to depopulate the Earth by using vaccines, alternative lifestyles, disease, abortion, and prison?

Considering Black people are the original homo sapiens of the Earth with an estimated 300,000+ years of history and are responsible for modern civilization; what kind of God allows the white community to assign a badge of dishonor to Black people? What kind of God allows white individuals to rewrite scriptures, create fake religious images, and incorrectly put a white face on God? White overseers must have their fingers crossed that honestly there is no God whatsoever so they can behave as god themselves. The author concurs that if there is a God then such established world-renowned holocaustic wickedness should be eternally punished for all the victims and world to see.

In essence, if the pinnacle of white society's power manifests in: egregious racial violence and discrimination, promoting perilous alternative lifestyles, utilizing targeted abortion for zero-growth agendas, producing morally bankrupt television content contrary to any righteous higher-being, developing and deploying ethnic bioweapons and atomic bombs, purging Black communities, perpetuating ceaseless wars, and wreaking havoc on the environment—then, for the sake of global posterity encompassing all living beings, it should be left to God to determine who is deemed worthy of being an Earthling. Given their extensively documented history of genocide, briefly discussed in this book, divine intervention and judgment should not favor either the mark of the beast or the homicidal rule of whites, now seemingly inseparable.

Here is a chart that recaps *Black American History* and summarizes the Black Genocide:

Leftist Weapons and Tactics	Far-right Weapons and Tactics
Hollywood is used to promote incompatible liberal itineraries, distort Black image and bribe blacks to advance leftist agendas	As the 6th leading cause of death for Black Americans, law enforcement is used to abuse and kill Black citizens and help fill up prisons. **Genocide**
Supports eugenics and sponsors targeted birth control and abortions, all used to suppress Black birthrate. Genocide	Originated eugenics. Also uses mass incarceration to lower Black birthrate and provide cheap labor—slavery and **Genocide**
Utilize homosexuality to destroy the Black family. Also used to reduce Black birthrate and depopulate by both decreasing fertility rates and increasing AIDS—thus lowering lifespan. Genocide	Originated abortions. AIDS was introduced under the Reagan Administration and combined with crack cocaine, amounting to biological and chemical attacks on Blacks. **Genocide**
Currently control and finance "Black" organizations plus procure and introduce Black leadership. Treats gang-banging, crime-promoting rappers like leaders	Historically imprisoned, exiled and outright murdered Black leadership and destroyed Black organizations. Treats gang-banging, crime-promoting rappers like leaders
Use Benign Neglect to politically ignore Black interests. Uses racial slurs	Passionately uses racial slurs, harassment and mental torment, "nigger go back to Africa" and "slavery did you a favor"
Oppose adequate reparations	Oppose adequate reparations
Rewrite Black history by producing false movies featuring whites doing what Blacks actually did, such as build pyramids, or replace historical iconic Black figures like King Tut, Hannibal and Jesus Christ through whitewashed media	Deny Black history, "you people were just primitive monkeys until you met whites." Additionally, deny systemic racism or white privilege exists. Also uses self-blame and false claims like "Blacks are more racist than whites"

Leftist Weapons and Tactics	Far-right Weapons and Tactics
Use court system and media to legitimize actions and leftist agendas	Use court system and media to legitimize actions and far-right agendas
Use Uncle Toms to advance alien agendas antithetical to Black interests	Use Uncle Toms to impersonate white supremacists who openly despise Blacks
Use Pseudoscience to justify abortions, homosexuality and targeting children	Use Pseudoscience to claim Blacks are genetically inferior and prone to violence
Use rap music to promote pathology, drug and alcohol use. Also used to popularize criminal activity and normalize prison. Rap is used to legitimize black street gangs who are then used as instruments of fratricide. These deadly gangs kill more Blacks than racist groups such as the KKK. Genocide	Historically and currently uses violent vigilantes like the KKK, domestic terrorists, confederates, white nationalists, armed militias and other white supremacist groups to propagate hate, kill and terrorize Blacks. Normalize these hate groups by labeling them "patriotic" and "conservative"
Ignore professional Black economists and dedicated leadership. Instead, discuss financial agendas with unintelligent, despicable, foul-mouth lowlifes and active gang members who perform atrocious rap music. Seek endorsements from vile rappers to anoint ineffective Black leadership.	Ignore professional Black economists and dedicated leadership. Instead, discuss financial agendas with unintelligent, despicable, foul-mouth lowlifes and active gang members who perform atrocious rap music. Seek endorsements from vile rappers to anoint ineffective Black leadership.
Economically disenfranchise Blacks by undermining self-sufficiency and redirecting them towards white dependency	Economically disenfranchise Blacks through hiring practices, destroy Black economic zones and businesses with urban renewal and violence

If you liked this book, kindly leave a review.

Your support helps to publish more books like this.

https://www.amazon.com/review/create-review/?ie=UTF8&channel=glance-detail&asin=B0CDJC7NH6

End Notes

[1] The American Directory of Certified Uncle Toms, CBIA Publishing, 2002, page 11

[2] *Ghetto Informant Program of 1967,* Moorish Harem, June 26, 2015, http://moorishharem.com/the-ghetto-informant-program-of-1967/ see also Simeon Booker, *Key Black Extremists' Stalked, Wiretapped, Harassed by FBI:* Report," *Jet*, 17 June 1976, Colbert I. King, *"Sneaking and Peeking—Then and Now," Washington Post*, 8 June 2002, p. A21

[3] Key Black Extremists' Stalked, Wiretapped, Harassed by FBI: Report, Simeon Booker, June 17, 1976, Jet Magazine

[4] Ibid

[5] *Understanding Jim Crow,* David Pilgram, *PM Press,* 2015, see also The *Rise and Fall of Jim Crow,* Richard Wormser, St. Martin's Publishing Group, 2014

[6] Benign Neglect on Race is Proposed by Moynihan, Peter Kihss, 1970, The New York Times

[7] *An Entire Village owned By Black People was destroyed to Build Central Park,* Heather Gilligan, Timeline, February 22, 2017, https://timeline.com/black-village-destroyed-central-park-6356723113fa?gi=b4ff97f73281 see also *New York Destroyed a Village Full of African-American Landowners to Create Central Park,* Barbara Speed, City Metric, March 30, 2015, https://www.citymetric.com/skylines/new-york-destroyed-village-full-african-american-landowners-create-central-park-893

[8] The Federal Government was the Primary Catalyst of Housing Segregation, Foundation for Economic Education, March 14, 2019, https://fee.org/articles/the-federal-government-was-the-primary-catalyst-of-housing-segregation/?gclid=CjwKCAjwxqX4BRBhEiwAYtJX7cCOkQfnGmhEa1PR2eM6yB4g349m_ECPur2LOwfZlrmTH1tLMSAJXBoCk3EQAvD_BwE see also A 'Forgotten History' of How the U.S. Government Segregated America, Terry Gross, May 3, 2017

[9] The Color of Law, Richard Rothstein, Liveright Publishing Corporation, 2017, The author also noted how Blacks and Mexicans were treated by the Ford plant that employed them, greeting them with a sign saying "No Mexican or Black Workers Wanted." They made exceptions for those with needed trades and talents. He also wrote "To ensure that no African Americans migrated to Richmond unless they were essential to the war effort, the city's police stopped African American men on the street and then arrested and jailed them if they couldn't prove they were employed," page 4, Google Books, https://www.google.com/books/edition/The_Color_of_Law_A_Forgotten_History_of/SdtDDQAAQBAJ?hl=en&gbpv=1

[10] Redlining Legacy: Maps are Gone, But the Problem Hasn't Disappeared, Khristopher J. Brooks, CBS News, June 12, 2020, https://www.cbsnews.com/news/redlining-what-is-history-mike-bloomberg-comments/

[11] *Billions Stolen From Black Families by Predatory Lending,* The Real News Network, June 20, 2019, YouTube video

[12] *Uprooted: Urban renewal in Asheville,* Thomas Calder, March 8, 2020 Mountain X, https://mountainx.com/news/uprooted-urban-renewal-in-asheville/ see also Systematic Inequality, Angela Hanks, Danyelle Christian E. Weller, February 21, 2018, Center For American Progress, https://www.americanprogress.org/issues/race/reports/2018/02/21/447051/systematic-inequality/ see also Red lining New York Times https://www.nytimes.com/2017/06/20/books/review/richard-rothstein-color-of-law-forgotten-history.html

[13] *Top Infrastructure Official Explains how America used Highways to Destroy Black Neighborhoods,* Alan Pyke, March 31, 2016, *Think Progress,* https://archive.thinkprogress.org/top-infrastructure-official-explains-how-america-used-highways-to-destroy-black-neighborhoods-96c1460d1962/ see also *Interstate Injustice: Plowing Highways Through Minority Neighborhoods-Updated,* April 7, 2018, *Panethos,* https://panethos.wordpress.com/2018/04/07/interstate-injustice-plowing-highways-through-minority-neighborhoods/ and *New Highways Have Destroyed Black Neighborhoods for Decades, Transportation Secretary Anthony Foxx Hopes to Fix it,* Manny Otiko, March 31, 2016, *Atlanta Black Star,* https://atlantablackstar.com/2016/03/31/new-highways-have-destroyed-black-neighborhoods-for-decades-transportation-secretary-anthony-foxx-hopes-to-fix-it/

[14] W.E.B. Du Bois, Documenting the American South, https://docsouth.unc.edu/nc/dubois/summary.html#:~:text=Writing%20in%201912%2C%20Du%20Bois,at%20a%20colored%20haberdashery%20and see also https://www.theroot.com/the-other-black-wall-streets-1823010812

[15] *Maggie L. Walker,* by Arlisha R. Norwood, 2017, *National Women's History Month,* https://www.womenshistory.org/education-resources/biographies/maggie-l-walker see also Black History Month: Maggie L. Walker Female Banking Pioneer, February 21, 2019, Yahoo Finance YouTube channel

[16] *Uprooted: Urban renewal in Asheville,* Thomas Calder, March 8, 2020, Mountain X, https://mountainx.com/news/uprooted-urban-renewal-in-asheville/

[17] *Chuck D Calls Out Maury Povich and Jerry Springer for Exploiting Young Black People* https://www.complex.com/music/2019/11/chuck-d-accuses-maury-povich-jerry-springer-exploiting-black-people

[18] *How cop shows serve to reinforce the racism at the heart of our culture,* July 24, 2020, *The Conversation,* https://theconversation.com/how-cop-shows-serve-to-reinforce-the-racism-at-the-heart-of-our-culture-142506

[19] *Why B.E.T. Sucks,* Holly Bass, March 8, 1996, *Washington City Paper,* https://www.washingtoncitypaper.com/news/article/13010336/why-bet-sucks During an interview in 2010, BET co-founder Sheila Johnson stated she was "ashamed" of what the network has become. "I don't watch it. I suggest to my kids that they don't watch it." BET has never lived up to its potential and under white rule it never will. *Sheila Johnson Slams BET,* April 29, 2010, *The Daily Beast*

[20] *The Secret Meeting That Changed Rap Music and Destroyed a Generation*, author anonymous, http://court.rchp.com/history/racial-bias-in-mass-media/the-secret-meeting-that-changed-rap-

music-and-destroyed-a-generation/ see also The Secret Meeting that Destroyed Hip Hop, Black Angel Media channel, https://www.youtube.com/watch?v=nqOSkfUw6Rw YouTube video

[21] Page 237 The American Directory of Certified Uncle Toms

[22] *Reebok drops Rick Ross over lyric apology fallout,* Lawrence Crook III, April 12, 2013, CNN https://www.cnn.com/2013/04/11/showbiz/reebok-drops-rick-ross/index.html He repeatedly apologized but to no avail

[23] *Unsung: The Story of the Geto Boys,* Willie D Live channel, https://www.youtube.com/watch?v=9VfDh43LU7g YouTube video. Willie D participated in making music that contributed to Black pathology, but he has redeemed himself many times over with commentary that is often well spoken, motivating, informative and pro-Black.

[24] HSM, Largest Crew Takedown In Hip Hop History? They Were Recreating Unsolved Crime Scenes In Their Music Videos! https://www.worldstarhiphop.com/videos/video.php?v=wshhJMGb9c1XVnmAk71j see also *Rap Music is a Government Conspiracy to Kill Blacks,* Bear Farrar, YouTube video, https://www.youtube.com/watch?time_continue=2&v=-mfvf7E7J7E&feature=emb_title

[25] Criminal Justice Fact Sheet, NAACP, https://www.naacp.org/criminal-justice-fact-sheet/ see also Federal Bureau of Prisons, Inmate Race, https://www.bop.gov/about/statistics/statistics_inmate_race.jsp see also *A Black teen didn't do her online schoolwork during the pandemic. A judge sent her to juvenile detention,* Jodi S. Cohen, *Insider,* July 14, 2020, Yahoo News https://www.yahoo.com/news/black-teen-didnt-her-online-194300056.html

[26] *FBI Planned to Push Pierce as Rival to King: Young N.Y. Lawyer was Viewed as More Pliable Black Leader,* Ronald J. Ostrow and Douglas Frantz, August 29, 1989, *Los Angeles Times* https://www.latimes.com/archives/la-xpm-1989-08-29-mn-1199-story.html

[27] *War at Home,* Brian Glick, 1989, South End Press

[28] The Spingarn Medal, NAACP, https://www.naacp.org/awards/spingarn-medal/

[29] *Stolen Legacy: The Egyptian Origins of Western Philosophy,* Page. 14, George G.M. James, 2002, African American Images, first published in 1954, see also *An Investigation into the Death of Professor George G.M. James,* Charles D. Johnson, December 29, 2015, Medium, https://medium.com/@afrdiaspora/an-investigation-in-the-death-of-professor-george-g-m-james-cfe4401be83e

[30] Egypt Search, December 12, 2009, http://www.egyptsearch.com/forums/ultimatebb.cgi?ubb=next_topic;f=8;t=006610;go=older

[31] The white people now in Egypt are the worse when it comes to cultural misappropriation. They arrived in Egypt around 649AD or about 1400 years ago. The pyramids have been there for almost 5,000 years and somehow they claim to have built them! Like other white Arabs in the so-called Middle East and North Africa they tell the native Black people that slavery is their only history going back to antiquity. That is also taught in their schools. In 1983 Columbia Pictures made a film titled *Sadat,* a miniseries about the life of Anwar Sadat with Louis Gossett Jr. playing the part of Sadat, both Black men. Egypt was so furious that Gossett was playing the part they filed a lawsuit against Columbia, see *Because they don't like the Sadat film,*

Egyptians ban all Columbia Pictures, Wadie Kirolos, February 27, 1984, UPI, https://www.upi.com/Archives/1984/02/27/Because-they-dont-like-Sadat-film-Egyptians-ban-all-Columbia-Pictures/9075446706000/

[32] *How Europeans evolved white skin,* Ann Gibbs, April 2, 2015, *Science Magazine,* http://www.sciencemag.org/news/2015/04/how-europeans-evolved-white-skin The article dates modern white Homo sapiens at around 8,000 years old and says Blacks left Africa and went to Europe 40,000 years ago. The more common estimate for white Europeans being on Earth is around 5,000 years, see *White Europeans 'only evolved 5,500 years ago after food habits changed,'* August 31, 2009, *Daily Mail,* http://www.dailymail.co.uk/sciencetech/article-1210056/White-Europeans-evolved-5-500-years-ago-food-habits-changed.html There are few modern innovations in Europe 5-10 thousand years ago so the next best thing for the "master race" is to steal credit from Africans to offset facts contradicting white superiority.

[33] *The African Origins of Mathematics,* African Creation Energy channel, YouTube video, https://www.youtube.com/watch?v=rYny1iQ_1r8&t=193s see also *The African Origins of Writing/Mathematics & Semitic Languages,* Nile Valley History channel, YouTube video, https://www.youtube.com/watch?v=6ZoOQvb_wc0 see also *African Origins of Math Dr Ron Eglash Pt1,* Black History Walks channel, YouTube video, https://www.youtube.com/watch?v=LXRvwk12atw see also *Ancient Math of Ethiopia - Amazing Methods of Calculation.flv, BBC,* Ethiopian World Net channel, YouTube video, November 12, 2010, https://www.youtube.com/watch?v=uXOTKidm7A0

[34] Ruins of Empires and the Law of Nature: The Ruins, or Meditation on the Revolutions of Empires, C.F. Volney, 1789, Kush, 1983, When Africa Ruled the World, P. 14, Dr. Rufus Jimerson

[35] *Did the ancient Greeks get their ideas from the Africans?* The Kemetic Mystery System, Josh Clark, *How Stuff Works,* https://history.howstuffworks.com/history-vs-myth/greek-philosophers-african-tribes1.htm see also *Stolen Legacy: Greek Philosophy is Stolen African Philosophy,* George G. M. James, Pan African, http://www.jpanafrican.org/ebooks/eBook%20Stolen%20Legacy.pdf

[36] *15 Things You Did Not Know About The Moors of Spain,* Black History Studies, https://blackhistorystudies.com/resources/resources/15-facts-on-the-moors-in-spain/ see also *The Black Africans Who Ruled Europe from 711 to 1789,* Ujamma team, https://ujamaalive.africa/history/the-black-africans-who-ruled-europe-from-711-to-1789/

[37] *5 Eurocentric Myths About Black History, and Pictures that Disproves Them,* A Moore, January 9, 2015, *Atlantic Black Star,* https://atlantablackstar.com/2015/01/09/5-eurocentric-myths-about-black-history-and-pictures-that-disprove-them/ This link provides must read information!

[38] Cesarean Section-A Brief History, U.S. National Library of Medicine, https://www.nlm.nih.gov/exhibition/cesarean/part2.html

[39] *Guide to Traditional African Board Games,* Anouk Zijlma, August 20, 2019, The Spruce Crafts, https://www.thesprucecrafts.com/games-played-in-africa-1454491#:~:text=Mancala%20is%20one%20of%20the,%2C%20omweso%2C%20enkeshui%20or%20aweet.

[40]Ancient Egypt: Birthplace of the Modern Calendar, Thought Co, https://www.thoughtco.com/ancient-egypt-birthplace-of-modern-calendar-43706

[41]*Black Jesus from Egyptian American Coptic Christian's View, W/Mariam,* 2017, Blog Post Radio, https://www.blogtalkradio.com/thegistoffreedom/2016/09/06/black-jesus-from-egyptian-american-coptic-christians-view-w-mariam see also The Real Face of Jesus, https://www.earthlymission.com/the-real-face-of-jesus/ see *also Did you know? The image of "Jesus" is really based on the likeness of Cesare Borgia?* Warriors of the Ruwach, https://warriorsoftheruwach.com/en/cesare-borgia see also *White Supremacy Shaped Christianity, Researchers Say,* Carol Kuruvilla, *HuffPost* July 26, 2020, Yahoo https://www.yahoo.com/huffpost/white-supremacy-christianity-robert-jones-160000229.html

[42]*Church Unearthed in Ethiopia Rewrites the History of Christianity in Africa,* Andrew Lawler, December 10, 2019, *Smithsonian Magazine,* https://www.smithsonianmag.com/history/church-unearthed-ethiopia-rewrites-history-christianity-africa-180973740/ see also *Ethiopia in the Bible,* Ethiopian History, https://ethiopianhistory.com/Ethiopia_in_the_Bible/

[43]*African American Life in the Rural South,* 1900-1950, R. Douglas Hurt, University of Missouri Press, 2003

[44]The Scramble for Africa, White Man's Conquest of the Dark Continent From 1876 to 1912, Thomas Parkenham, 1992, Harper Collins

[45] UN on genocide prevention https://www.un.org/en/genocideprevention/genocide.shtml If you combine the fact that homosexuality repeatedly meets the UN definition for genocide with the Census showing a growth rate of 0.5 percent over 20 years it further confirms genocide. On page 3 the U.S. census data shows Blacks were 12.9% in 2000, and 13.6% in 2010. See *The Black Population: 2010,* https://www.census.gov/prod/cen2010/briefs/c2010br-06.pdf By 2020 the Black population decreased from 13.6% to 13.4% without any fanfare, see *United States Census Quick Facts,* https://www.census.gov/quickfacts/fact/table/US/PST045219 This shows that Blacks haven't grown even 1% over 20 years, GENOCIDE. See also *'Black Americans' mortality rate has been disproportionately high in 2020 — even without coronavirus deaths,* Kathryn Krawczyk, September 18, 2020, *The Week,* https://news.yahoo.com/black-americans-mortality-rate-disproportionately-210400559.html

[46]*Ring the Alarm, The Crisis of Black Youth Suicide in America,* A Report to Congress From The Congressional Black Caucus, https://watsoncoleman.house.gov/uploadedfiles/full_taskforce_report.pdf

[47]*Award Stripped From Lesbian Civil Rights Icon Angela Davis,* Neal Broverman, January 9, 2019, *Advocate* https://www.advocate.com/people/2019/1/09/award-stripped-lesbian-civil-rights-icon-angela-davis

[48]*Atlanta's HIV epidemic compared to third world African countries,* Dave Huddleston, November 30, 2018, WSB-TV, https://www.wsbtv.com/news/2-investigates/atlantas-hiv-epidemic-compared-to-third-world-african-countries/263337845/ see also *Doctor Said He Heard 70% of Black Women in Fulton County Georgia are HIV Positive,* https://www.worldstarhiphop.com/videos/video.php?v=wshhf3LyHAWba0PEs95A In 2008

CNN had the audacity to do a documentary that claimed AIDS was a "Black people's disease." Black AIDS Epidemic AIDS in America Today is a Black Disease, July 31, 2008, World Star Hip Hop, https://www.worldstarhiphop.com/videos/video.php?v=wshhz6pQ2ysYx5iHM97a

[49]*Anal intercourse and fecal incontinence: Evidence from the 2009-2010 National Health and Nutrition Examination Survey,* January 12, 2016, National Center for Biotechnology Information, https://www.ncbi.nlm.nih.gov/pmc/articles/PMC5231615/ see also *The awful secret about the consequences of homosexual (gay) sex,* Australian Federation for the Family, https://www.ausfamily.org/resources/sexual-behaviour/the-gay-sex-secret-homosexuals-want-no-one-to-know

[50]*The gay bowel syndrome: a common problem of homosexual patients in the emergency department,* National Center of Biotechnology Information, September 9, 1980, https://pubmed.ncbi.nlm.nih.gov/6893530/

[51]U.S. *Officials Push for Expelling Suspected Chinese Spies at Media Outlets,* Edward Bong and Julian E. Barnes, March 26, 2020, *New York Times,* https://www.nytimes.com/2020/03/26/us/politics/coronavirus-china-spies.html see also *U.S. officially warns China is launching cyber attacks to steal corona virus research,* Alex Marquardt, Kylie Atwood, Zachery Cohen, March 13, 2020 CNN https://www.cnn.com/2020/05/13/politics/us-china-hacking-coronavirus-warning/index.html see also *Russia Reportedly Offered Bounties To Taliban To Kill U.S. Troops,* June 29, 2020, NPR, https://www.npr.org/2020/06/29/884551328/russia-reportedly-offered-bounties-to-taliban-to-kill-u-s-troops

[52]*5horrifying ways enslaved African men were sexually exploited and abused by their white masters,* Elizabeth Ofosuah Johnson, October 11, 2018, Face2Face Africa, https://face2faceafrica.com/article/5-horrifying-ways-enslaved-african-men-were-sexually-exploited-and-abused-by-their-white-masters/2 Raping male slaves was just as common as raping Black women

Here are some of the demographics and economic characteristics of America's gay couples," Andy Kiersz, June 27, 2015, *Business Insider*, https://www.businessinsider.com/census-data-on-gay-households-2015-6 see also "*Married gay couples beat straight couples in income"* Kurtis Alexander and Sarah Ravani, September 12, 2016, *Seattle Times,* https://www.seattletimes.com/nation-world/married-gay-couples-beat-straight-couples-in-income/#:~:text=The%20federal%20agency's%20first%2Dever,were%20raking%20in%20nearly%20%24275%2C000. see also *Blacks only racial group still making less than in 2000,* September 17, 2017, The Gazette, https://www.thegazette.com/subject/news/business/blacks-only-racial-group-still-making-less-than-in-2000-20170915 and *African Americans the only racial group earning less than in 2000,* Heather Long, September 17, 2017, *Chicago Tribune* https://www.chicagotribune.com/business/ct-african-americans-income-census-20170918-story.html

[53]210 reasons for decline of Roman Empire https://courses.washington.edu/rome250/gallery/ROME%20250/210%20Reasons.htm Homosexuality isn't at the top of the list for empire destruction and it is not at the bottom but

most of all, it is on the list. Also, how politically correct does the list have to be in order to exist? If someone placed homosexuality as the number one reason there might be consequences. The list is also in alphabetical order meaning the order of the list isn't based on the impact each reason had on the Roman Empire. Usually when great empires crumble it is due to a list of reasons, not just a single factor. A list of reasons for Black decline will be rampant homosexuality, mass incarceration, abortions, crime, drugs, poverty, racism, suicide and more. Homosexuality has never single-handedly destroyed a civilization but as shown hypothetically it can. There is always a list of reasons for decline but having a list of reasons doesn't give homosexuality a pass, instead it shows that the combination of it with other serious problems can diminish or bring down empires and communities. If homosexuality was epidemic then the fall of the Roman Empire was guaranteed to eventually happen. See *Fall of Roman Empire caused by 'contagion of homosexuality,'* April 8, 2011, *The Telegraph,* United Kingdom, https://www.telegraph.co.uk/news/worldnews/europe/italy/8438210/Fall-of-Roman-Empire-caused-by-contagion-of-homosexuality.html

[54] *Target Promotes LGBTQ Pride Month Products for Children,* Gavi Greenspan, June 18, 2018, CNS News, https://www.cnsnews.com/news/article/gavi-greenspan/target-promotes-lgbtq-pride-month-products-children

[55] *Urinals banned in Portland municipal building to 'remove arbitrary barriers'* in gender-neutral quest, Dave Urbanski, September 30, 2019, The Blaze, https://www.theblaze.com/news/urinals-banned-in-portland-municipal-building-to-remove-arbitrary-barriers-in-gender-neutral-quest see also The end of urinals in the Portland building, KGW News channel, September 20, 2019, YouTube video, https://www.youtube.com/watch?v=OmCnX9F_-Sw) Man gets 16 years in prison for burning a rainbow flag, see *"Man sentenced to 16 years for burning church's pride flag,"* Madison Dibble, December 19, 2019, *Washington Examiner,* https://www.washingtonexaminer.com/news/man-sentenced-to-16-years-in-prison-for-burning-churchs-pride-flag see also *Man sentenced to 16 years in prison for burning stolen LGBT outside of strip club,* Clark Mindock, December 20, 2019, *Independent,* https://www.independent.co.uk/news/world/americas/burn-flag-lgbt-man-sentenced-prison-adolfo-martinez-ames-iowa-a9255316.html

[56] *Not using transgender pronouns could get you fired,* Joe Tacopino, May 19, 2016, *New York Post,* https://nypost.com/2016/05/19/city-issues-new-guidelines-on-transgender-pronouns/

[57] *Bathhouse Issue Difficult for Gay Community,* Jerry Schwartz, November 1, 1985, *AP News,* https://apnews.com/341795579f9231f8bb2472c61d91ae91 "its prime business, however, is providing a place for sex." In fact, in California it is mandatory for second graders to visit gay bars and drink beer! (*California School System to Feature Mandatory 2nd Grade Field Trips to Gay Bars,* June 28, 2019, *The Babylon Bee,* https://babylonbee.com/news/california-public-schools-mandate-field-trips-to-gay-bars-for-second-graders

[58] *Palm Springs police chief resigns over gay sex sting,* Phil Willon, January 11, 2011, *Los Angeles Times,* https://www.latimes.com/archives/la-xpm-2011-jan-11-la-me-palm-springs-20110111-story.html

[59] Netflix's Self-Made*: Incredible true story and controversy behind Madam C.J. Walker show,* March 26, 2020, *Mirror,* https://www.mirror.co.uk/tv/tv-news/netflixs-self-made-incredible-true-21758876

[60] *Gallop Poll Finds People of Color More Likely To Identify As LGBT,* October 19, 2012, Huffington Post, https://www.huffpost.com/entry/black-gays-lgbt-community_n_1989859 Blacks identify as homosexual more than any other group, see also *Homosexual Bakeries Discriminate Against Heterosexuals,* Gary Demar, December 20, 2014, *Godfather Politics,* https://godfatherpolitics.com/homosexual-bakeries-discriminate-heterosexuals/ see also *Straight WNBA Star: Lesbian Culture Broke My Spirit,* February 21, 2017, *New York Post,* https://nypost.com/2017/02/21/retired-wnba-star-i-was-tormented-for-not-being-gay/

[61] *The Effects of Abortion On The Black Community,* June, 2015, *Policy Report,* https://docs.house.gov/meetings/JU/JU10/20171101/106562/HHRG-115-JU10-Wstate-ParkerS-20171101-SD001.pdf

[62] Abortion: *The overlooked tragedy for Black Americans,* February 25, 2020, *Arizona Capital Times,* https://azcapitoltimes.com/news/2020/02/25/abortion-the-overlooked-tragedy-for-black-americans/ In New York City thousands more Black babies are aborted than born. "Between 2012 and 2016 Black mothers terminated 136,426 pregnancies and gave birth to 118,127 babies." See *Let's Talk About the Black Abortion Rate,* Jason L. Riley, July 10, 2018, *Wall Street Journal,* https://www.wsj.com/articles/lets-talk-about-the-black-abortion-rate-1531263697

[63] American Progress https://www.americanprogress.org/issues/race/reports/2018/04/18/449774/racism-evergreen-toxin-killing-black-mothers-infants/ see also Dr. Martin Luther King, Jr. "Where Do We Go From Here?" Boston: Beacon Press, 2010, p. 73.

Michael C. Lu and Neal Halfon, "Racial and ethnic disparities in birth outcomes: A life-course perspective," *Maternal and Child Health Journal* 7 (2003): 13–30

Lisa Rosenthal and Marci Lobe, "Explaining racial disparities in adverse birth outcomes: Unique sources of stress for Black American women," *Social Science & Medicine* 72 (2011): 977–98 *Fighting at Birth: Eradicating the Black-White Infant Mortality Gap,* Samuel DuBois Cook Center on Social Equity at Duke University, Imari Z. Smith, Keisha L. Bentley-Edwards, Salimah El-Amin and William Darity Jr., "*New Report: Why the Black-White Infant Mortality Gap Exists and How to Eradicate It,*" March 28, 2018, https://today.duke.edu/2018/03/new-report-why-black-white-infant-mortality-gap-exists-and-how-eradicate-it and https://socialequity.duke.edu/wp-content/uploads/2019/12/Eradicating-Black-Infant-Mortality-March-2018.pdf

Margaret Sanger First American Birth Control Clinic, (The Brownsville Clinic) 1916, Rainey Horwitz, October 11, 2019, The Embryo Project Encyclopedia, https://embryo.asu.edu/pages/first-american-birth-control-clinic-brownsville-clinic-1916 Sanger admitted to wanting to exterminate Blacks, https://www.dailysignal.com/2015/07/22/13-things-you-probably-dont-know-about-planned-parenthood-founder-margaret-sanger/ and *Margaret Sanger wanted to exterminate Negros,* September 21, 2015, *Liberty Under Attack,* YouTube, https://www.youtube.com/watch?v=DWtn4OUgp1Y&list=LLqws64u1vfjtlYvEg2hLftA&in

dex=1 see also *New study reveals that Black newborns are more likely to survive under care of Black doctor,* September 18, 2020, *CBS News, Yahoo,* https://www.yahoo.com/news/study-reveals-black-newborns-more-192613744.html

[64] *Italian politician Sara Cunial accuses Bill Gates and the corrupt parliament,* Parents for Healthcare Rights channel, May 18, 2020, YouTube video, https://www.youtube.com/watch?v=2NGMJDz7MFs

[65] *Bill Gates on the Search for a Vaccine: Dr. Sanjay Gupta's coronavirus podcast for June 30, 2020,* CNN https://www.cnn.com/2020/06/30/health/gupta-coronavirus-podcast-wellness-june-30/index.html see also *Genocide News,* https://genocide.news/2020-06-30-black-people-are-first-targets-bill-gates-vaccines.html

[66] *Genocide News,* https://genocide.news/2020-06-30-black-people-are-first-targets-bill-gates-vaccines.html see also *The Long Strange History of Bill Gates Population Control Conspiracy Theories,* Investigations, Kathryn Joyce, May 12, 2020, https://www.typeinvestigations.org/investigation/2020/05/12/the-long-strange-history-of-bill-gates-population-control-conspiracy-theories/

[67] *Prince Williams Is Worried There Are Just Too Many People In The World,* Josh Lowe, November 3, 2017, *Newsweek,* https://www.newsweek.com/prince-charles-prince-william-elephants-population-climate-change-700696 see also *Why Prince Williams Speech is Receiving a Lot of Backlash,* Olivia Bahou, November 3, 2017, Instyle https://www.instyle.com/news/prince-william-speech-overpopulation-backlash

[68] *African Women Injected With Vaccines Laced With Anti-Fertility Hormones,* Christina England, December 10, 2014, *Go Midwife* https://gomidwife.com/wp-content/uploads/2015/09/African-Women-Injected-With-Vaccines-Laced-with-Anti-fertility-Hormones.pdf see also *A mass sterilization exercise: Kenyan doctors find anti-fertility agent in UN tetanus vaccine,* November 8, 2014, https://en.preprod.reseauinternational.net/mass-sterilization-exercise-kenyan-doctors-find-anti-fertility-agent-un-tetanus-vaccine/

[69] CDC-funded study confirms flu shots linked to spontaneous abortions…vaccine experts rush to explain away the findings, September 13, 2017, Mike Adams, Vaccine News https://vaccines.news/2017-09-13-cdc-funded-study-confirms-flu-shots-linked-to-spontaneous-abortions-vaccine-experts-rush-to-explain-away-the-findings.html

[70] *French doctors apologize for comments on testing a COVID-19 vaccine in Africa, prompting outrage on social media,* Wilson Wong, April 7, 2020, *NBC News,* https://www.nbcnews.com/news/nbcblk/french-doctor-apologizes-comments-testing-covid-19-vaccine-africa-prompting-n1177991

[71] Robert F. Kennedy Jr. and Children's Health Defense Issue Report Regarding New Evidence of Ongoing Corruption and Scientific Misconduct at CDC, September 18, 2017, Children's Health Defense https://childrenshealthdefense.org/press-release/robert-f-kennedy-jr-world-mercury-project-issue-report-regarding-new-evidence-ongoing-corruption-scientific-misconduct-cdc/

[72] *CDC Whistleblower Revealed,* Autism Media Channel, August 22, 2014, YouTube https://www.youtube.com/watch?v=sGOtDVilkUc&feature=youtu.be&list=UUfIZ2PofuUg

EM79W3fOc6Mg and *Whistleblower Claims CDC Cover up Data Showing Vaccine-Autism Link,* Alice Park, August 28, 2014 https://time.com/3208886/whistleblower-claims-cdc-covered-up-data-showing-vaccine-autism-link/

[73] *CDC knew MMR vaccines caused autism! Whistleblower revealed,* Prison Planet InfoWars channel, https://www.youtube.com/watch?v=Z2CBd2H9H5I YouTube video, see also *Baby Killing Vaccine: Is it Being Stealth Tested?* James A. Miller, *The Eternal World Television Network,* https://www.ewtn.com/catholicism/library/babykilling-vaccine-is-it-being-stealth-tested-11055

[74] *U.S. Vaccine Court Has Paid over Three Billion Dollars to Vaccine-Injured Families,* October 4, 2016, *Project Censored* https://www.projectcensored.org/13-us-vaccine-court-paid-three-billion-dollars-vaccine-injured-families/?doing_wp_cron=1593727811.7131850719451904296875 see also *Was Lyme Disease Created As A Bioweapon?* Nathan Chandler, August 26, 2019, *How Stuff Works,* https://science.howstuffworks.com/science-vs-myth/what-if/lyme-disease-bioweapon.htm and *Pentagon May Have Released Weaponized Ticks That Helped Spread Lyme Disease: Investigation Ordered,* Aristos Georgiou July 7, 2019, *Newsweek,* https://www.newsweek.com/pentagon-weaponized-ticks-lyme-disease-investigation-1449737

[75] *When Forced Sterilization was Legal in the U.S,* Matthew Wills, August3, 2017, JStor Daily, https://daily.jstor.org/when-forced-sterilization-was-legal-in-the-u-s/

[76] *Mississippi Appendectomy: The decades long practice of sterilizing poor black women,* February 25, 2019, *The Black Detour,* https://theblackdetour.com/mississippi-appendectomy-the-decades-long-practice-of-sterilizing-poor-black-women/

[77] *Judge Offers Inmates Reduced Sentences in Exchange for Vasectomy,* Kalhan Rosenblatt, July 21, 2017, *NBC News,* https://www.nbcnews.com/news/us-news/judge-offers-inmates-reduced-sentences-exchange-vasectomy-n785256 see also N.C. Justice for Sterilization Victims Foundation https://files.nc.gov/ncdoa/JSV/JS-brochure.pdf see also *Inside the hidden campaign to forcibly sterilize thousands of inmates in California women's prisons,* Julia Naftulin, November 24, 2020, *Yahoo,* https://www.yahoo.com/news/inside-hidden-campaign-forcibly-sterilize-214500154.html

Reparations for Black people in this North Carolina city could be coming. Here's how Hayley Fowler, *Miami Herald,* July 10, 2020 https://www.yahoo.com/news/reparations-black-people-north-carolina-232350051.html

For eugenic sterilization victims, belated justice, Irin Carmon, June 27, 2014 http://www.msnbc.com/all/eugenic-sterilization-victims-belated-justice

When forced sterilization in the U.S. was legal, Matthew Willis, August 3, 2017 https://daily.jstor.org/when-forced-sterilization-was-legal-in-the-u-s/

The Supreme Court Ruling That Led To 70,000 Sterilizations March 7, 2016 https://www.npr.org/sections/health-shots/2016/03/07/469478098/the-supreme-court-ruling-that-led-to-70-000-forced-sterilizations

Forced sterilization programs in California once harmed thousands-particular Latinas, The Conversation https://theconversation.com/forced-sterilization-programs-in-california-once-harmed-thousands-particularly-latinas-92324

Eugenics: Compulsory Sterilization in 50 American States https://www.uvm.edu/~lkaelber/eugenics/

The U.S. Government's Role in Sterilizing Women of Color Nadra Kareem Nittle, January 9, 2020 https://www.thoughtco.com/u-s-governments-role-sterilizing-women-of-color-2834600

Thirteen ways of looking at Buck vs Bell, Michelle Oberman, February 2010 https://www.jstor.org/stable/42894126?mag=when-forced-sterilization-was-legal-in-the-u-s&seq=1#metadata_info_tab_contents

California Sterilized More People Than Any U.S. State But Has Yet to Compensate Victims, Natalie Degaldillo, August 7, 2017https://www.governing.com/topics/public-justice-safety/gov-sterilization-california-reparations-tennessee-eugenics.html

[78]*Black babies were once used as alligator and crocodile bait in America in the 1900s,* Mildred Europa Taylor, August 19, 2018, *Face 2 Face Africa,* https://face2faceafrica.com/article/black-babies-were-once-used-as-alligator-and-crocodile-bait-in-america-in-the-1900s see also *Why Florida banned its 'Gator Bait' cheer amid movement against racial injustice,* Tadd Haislop, *Sporting News,* https://www.sportingnews.com/ca/ncaa-football/news/florida-gator-bait-cheer-banned/1hqjrzwx2cvap1w08dvoa819rq

[79]*The Tuskegee Timeline, Center for Disease Control and Prevention,* https://www.cdc.gov/tuskegee/timeline.htm, see also Tuskegee Experiment: The Infamous Syphilis Study, Elizabeth Nix, July 29, 2019, History, https://www.history.com/news/the-infamous-40-year-tuskegee-study

[80] *Emerging Viruses,* Leonard Horowitz, 1996, Tetrahedron

[81]*Ex Mercenary claims South African group tried to spread AIDS,* Emma Graham Harrison, January 27, 2019, The Guardian, https://www.theguardian.com/world/2019/jan/27/south-african-intelligence-officers-spread-aids-black-communities

[82] Frontline, What happened in South Africa? PBS, https://www.pbs.org/wgbh/pages/frontline/shows/plague/sa/ see also Frontline interview of F.W. de Clerk, https://www.pbs.org/wgbh/pages/frontline/shows/plague/sa/deklerk.html see also Frontline interview Daan Goosen, https://www.pbs.org/wgbh/pages/frontline/shows/plague/sa/goosen.html see also Roodeplatt Research Laboratories, https://wikileaks.org/gifiles/attach/33/33200_Roodeplaat%20Research%20Laboratories.pdf

[83]*An Unreliable Narrator, A Trail Colder Than Pickled Herring: 'Cold Case Hammarskjöld'* Ella Taylor, August 15, 2019, NPR, https://www.npr.org/2019/08/15/750812549/an-unreliable-narrator-a-trail-colder-than-pickled-herring-cold-case-hammarskj-l see also Helen E. Purkitt, Stephen F. Burgess: *South Africa's Weapons of Mass Destruction.* Indiana University Press, Bloomington 2005 and Helen E. Purkitt, Stephen F. Burgess: *The Rollback of South Africa's Chemical and Biological Warfare Program,* Air University, Counter Proliferation Center, Maxwell Air Force Base, Alabama, 2001 see also *We deliberately spread AIDS in South Africa,* Baffour Ankomah, February 3, 2019, New African Magazine, https://newafricanmagazine.com/18285/ see also Frontline, *What happened in South Africa,*

PBS, https://www.pbs.org/wgbh/pages/frontline/shows/plague/sa/ see also MK-Ultra, August 21, 2018, History.com, A&E Television Network, https://www.history.com/topics/us-government/history-of-mk-ultra

[84] *The New Jim Crow,* Page 6, Michelle Alexander, 2010, New Press

[85]*Dark Alliance,* Gary Webb, Page 14, 1998, Steven Stories Press

[86] *How John Kerry exposed the Contra-cocaine scandal,* Robert Parry, October 25, 2004, Salon, https://www.salon.com/2004/10/25/contra/

[87] *Former DEA Agent Wants George H. Bush, Negroponte, and Other Higher-Ups Held Accountable for Illegal Drug Smuggling,* Greg Szymanski, Rense.com, https://rense.com//general69/eVE.HTM

[88] *Race and Slavery in the Middle East,* Bernard Lewis, 1990, Oxford University Press see also *Don't Believe the Hype,* Farai Chideya, 1995, Plume Publishing

[89] *Slavery By Another Name,* Douglas A. Blackmon, 2008, Vintage Books, see also *Twice the Work of Free Labor,* Alex Lichtenstein, 1996, Verso Publishing

[90]1870 Census Report, https://www2.census.gov/library/publications/decennial/1870/population/1870a-04.pdf#

[91]*At Least 2000 More Black Americans Were Lynched Than Previously Reported,* Sarah Ruiz-Grossman, *HuffPost,* June 17, 2020, https://www.yahoo.com/huffpost/lynchings-black-americans-reconstruction-eji-report-203530106.html Yahoo News, see also *EJI Releases New Report Documenting 2,000 More Lynchings of Black People by White Mobs,* https://eji.org/reports/reconstruction-in-america-overview/ Equal Justice Initiative see also S. Res. 39, (109th): Lynching victims Senate Apology Resolution, June 13, 2005, GovTrk, 109th https://www.govtrack.us/congress/bills/109/sres39/text

[92] *Sundown Towns,* James W. Loewen, 2005, New Press

[93] *The Devastation of Black Wall Street,* Kimberly Fain, July 5, 2017, *Jstor Daily,* https://daily.jstor.org/the-devastation-of-black-wall-street/

[94] *Rosewood Massacre,* History.com, July 16, 2020, A&E Publishers, https://www.history.com/topics/early-20th-century-us/rosewood-massacre

[95]*July 29, 1910: Slocum Massacre in Texas, an act of Genocide in East Texas,* E.R. Bills, 2014, History Press, Zinn Education Project, https://www.zinnedproject.org/news/tdih/slocum-massacre/ also *Look What Has Been Taken From Black Americans,* Trevon Logan and William Darity Jr., *Bloomberg,* September 21, 2020, https://www.yahoo.com/news/look-taken-black-americans-123004644.html

[96] *How 20,000 Blacks died through starvation and overwork in the 'Devils Punchbowl' labor camp in Mississippi,* Michael Eli Dokosi, November 4, 2019, *Face 2 Face Africa,* https://face2faceafrica.com/article/how-20000-blacks-died-through-starvation-and-overwork-in-the-devils-punchbowl-labour-camp-in-mississippi see also *20K Blacks Died In Concentration Camp Called The Devils Punchbowl in Natchez Mississippi,* October 25, 2016, *African Diaspora News Channel,* YouTube Video https://www.youtube.com/watch?v=_3XNFizwilc&t=7s

[97] *Slave Patrol,* Sally E. Hadden, 2001, Harvard University Press

[98]*A Brief History of Slavery and the origins of American Policing,* Victory E. Kappeler, Eastern Kentucky University, Police Study Online, https://plsonline.eku.edu/insidelook/brief-history-slavery-and-origins-american-policing There is a preponderance of evidence that law enforcement is being used to control and kill Black Americans. See *More video released of Black Indiana man getting mauled by police dog* (WARNING: GRAPHIC) https://www.msn.com/en-us/news/crime/more-video-released-of-black-indiana-man-getting-mauled-by-police-dog-warning-graphic/ar-BB17dUiw?li=BBnbfcL Three white police officers confronted a very drunk man accused of assault. The victim verbally objected to getting off his moped with the police standing right next to him. After a brief attempt to remove him from the moped, instead of using a taser or pepper spray, the police held the man by his arms and allowed a K9 to chew on his neck for over 30 seconds. All the cops were cleared by the department and the K9 officer was promoted after the event. This attempted murder and the department acquittal indicts far-right white power and the police as organized liars and criminals. In this next video the police officer allegedly put plastic down the victim's throat. The video clearly shows the cop continuing to pinch the victim's nose shut even after he is unconscious. The officer also taunted him while simultaneously murdering him. The officer wasn't arrested but the honorable cop who blew the whistle was fired! See https://www.yahoo.com/news/joliet-police-sgt-stripped-powers-231645533.html

This next link shows police shooting a man in his back even though he was compliant. The female officer was charged but thanks to a hung jury she never served any time in prison. The cop who shot him from point blank range received $57,000 a year in disability income because she claimed she was stressed out over being criminally charged for shooting an unarmed compliant man in the back. She walked free and received more income from the disability than her police salary, all for shooting a Black man. See *Ex-Cop getting 57k a year in disability due to stress caused by being charged with shooting unarmed man*, Bruce Vielmetti, *Milwaukee Journal Sentinel,* December 25, 2019
https://www.jsonline.com/story/news/local/milwaukee/2019/12/20/ex-brown-deer-cop-charged-shooting-gets-57-000-duty-disability/2703702001/

See also *Police: Sixth leading cause of death for young Black men, Michigan News,* August 5, 2019, University of Michigan, https://news.umich.edu/police-sixth-leading-cause-of-death-for-young-black-men/ see also *Study: Police Violence a Leading Cause of Death for Young Men,* Joseph P. Williams, August 5, 2019, https://www.usnews.com/news/healthiest-communities/articles/2019-08-05/police-violence-a-leading-cause-of-death-for-young-men With millions of people regularly dealing with police bias and racial abuse Attorney General William Barr denied systemic racism exists. Denial is a way to prevent having a serious conversation about racism so that it never gets addressed. See *Barr says he disagrees there's systemic racism in police departments* July 28, 2020, *Yahoo News Videos,* https://www.yahoo.com/news/barr-says-disagrees-systemic-racism-182106091.html

Police abuse in the U.S. is so renowned that Black Americans can get asylum all over the world, see *If Black Americans were to seek asylum, they could qualify,* Amali Tower, June 17, 2020, *Aljazeera,* https://www.aljazeera.com/indepth/opinion/black-americans-seek-asylum-easily-qualify-200614094252933.html Police often complain about citizens not complying, but they also have a problem with compliance, see *The NYPD Isn't Giving Critical Bodycam Footage to Officials Investigating Alleged Abuse,* Eric Umansky, July 3, 2020, ProPublica, https://www.propublica.org/article/the-nypd-isnt-giving-critical-bodycam-footage-to-officials-investigating-alleged-abuse

[99] *France has Assassinated 22 African Presidents Since 1963,* Takudzwa Hillary Chiwanza, June 29, 2019, *The African Exponent,* https://www.africanexponent.com/post/10487-france-has-always-carried-evil-imperialism-with-it See also *22 African Presidents have been Assassinated by France Since 1963,* May 25, 2019, *African Globe,* https://www.africanglobe.net/africa/22-african-presidents-assassinated-france-1963/ see also *The coup that set Ghana and Africa 50 years back,* Charles Quist-Adade, March 2, 2016, Pambazuka News, https://www.pambazuka.org/governance/coup-set-ghana-and-africa-50-years-back

[100] *Illicit financial flows have made Africa 'a net creditor to the world,'* 2013, *The Guardian,* https://www.theguardian.com/global-development/2013/may/29/illicit-financial-flows-africa-creditor see also *Nigeria says it has recovered 9.1 billion in stolen money and assets,* June 4, 2016, Reuters, https://uk.reuters.com/article/uk-nigeria-corruption-idUKKCN0YQ0GI see also *Did David Cameron say the UK would 'cease to exist' if it were looted like Nigeria?* August 22, 2017, *Africa Check,* https://africacheck.org/spot-check/did-david-cameron-say-uk-would-cease-to-exist-if-money-looted-from-nigeria-were-stolen-there/ That is only one country in Africa. He really said "if we had to return the money we stole then the UK would cease to exist." See also *Switzerland to return 321 million to Nigeria,* Kieron Monks, December 6, 2017, CNN, https://www.cnn.com/2017/12/06/africa/switzerland-returns-abacha-funds/index.html see *also Recovered stolen money to partly finance Nigeria's 23 billion budget-official,* Ismail Akwei, June 14, 2017, *Africa News,* http://www.africanews.com/2017/06/14/recovered-stolen-money-to-finance-part-of-nigeria-s-23b-budget-official// see *also U.S., Nigeria sign deal to return $309 million stolen by Abacha,* February 6, 2020, CGTN, https://newsaf.cgtn.com/news/2020-02-06/U-S-Nigeria-sign-deal-to-return-309-million-stolen-by-Abacha-NQvqgRm33q/index.html the returned money comes from a 20 year effort and amounts to pennies on the dollar. The theft amounted to 5 billion and the U.S. kept the rest. See also *How trillions of dollars were stolen by greedy African despots and kept in the West,* Ismail Akwei, June 5, 2019, Face 2 Face Africa, https://face2faceafrica.com/article/how-trillions-of-dollars-were-stolen-by-greedy-african-despots-and-kept-in-the-west

[101] *Western racism in the IMF and the World Bank,* Peter Baofu, September 8, 2011, http://www.pravdareport.com/opinion/columnists/09-08-2011/118684-imf_racism_world_bank-0/ and also *Report Details Racial Discrimination At World Bank,* Government Accountability Project, https://whistleblower.org/press/report-details-racial-discrimination-world-bank/ In 2008 out of 3500 employees there were only four Black Americans. "Racial discrimination is an ugly practice, wherever it happens, but it has a particularly corrosive impact on an institution that serves as the primary source of development finance for sub-Saharan Africa. How does an institution committed to fighting poverty in Africa as a major part of its mission explain systemically disadvantaging the people of Black

African heritage in its own ranks?" As one unnamed World Bank vice president volunteered in the Bank's diversity report, "We are not likely to treat our clients better than we treat one another." See *Racial Discrimination at the World Bank,* Bea Edwards, Emily Schwartz Greco, June 19, 2009, *Foreign Policy in Focus* https://fpif.org/racial_discrimination_at_the_world_bank/ see also *African Nations say They're being ripped off by Wall Street,* Alonso Soto, September 8, 2020, *Bloomberg,* https://www.yahoo.com/finance/news/borrowing-costs-africa-stars-victims-040000542.html The article discusses how African nations with good credit pay more for loans compared to European countries with poor credit

[102]*US 'extends sanctions against Zim,' says new government is a product of military coup-report,* February14, 2018, *News 24,* https://www.news24.com/Africa/Zimbabwe/us-extends-sanctions-against-zim-says-new-govt-is-a-product-of-a-military-coup-report-20180214 see also U.S. *Sanctions Policy in Sub Saharan Africa,* June 8, 2016, *United States Institute of Peace,* https://www.usip.org/publications/2016/06/us-sanctions-policy-sub-saharan-africa "Africa has been far and away the target of more sanctions from the UN, the European Union (EU), and the U.S. than any other continent."

[103] *Brain drain: a bane to Africa's potential* August 9, 2018, *Mo Ibrahim,* https://mo.ibrahim.foundation/news/2018/brain-drain-bane-africas-potential see also *African Brain Drain: Is there an alternative?* UNESCO Courier, https://en.unesco.org/courier/january-march-2018/african-brain-drain-there-alternative

[104] *France/Afrique : 14 African Countries Forced by France to Pay Colonial Tax For the Benefits of Slavery and Colonization,* July 29, 2020, CongoNews, MediaPart, https://blogs.mediapart.fr/jecmaus/blog/300114/franceafrique-14-african-countries-forced-france-pay-colonial-tax-benefits-slavery-and-colonization see also *The 11 Components of the French Colonial Tax in Africa,* May 1, 2017, Mr. Y, *Afrolegends,* https://afrolegends.com/2017/05/01/the-11-components-of-the-french-colonial-tax-in-africa/

[105] Haiti fought against slavery and won their freedom. Then France decided to charge them close to $20 billion dollars if they wanted to remain free. The debt was supposedly due because of the lost revenue from slavery, even though slavery was outlawed at the time. Haiti paid the crushing debt from 1825 to 1947. In 2004, a lawsuit launched by Haiti to recover the money was abandoned when France backed the overthrow of the government. See *France urged to repay Haiti billions paid for its independence,* 2010, *The Guardian,* https://www.theguardian.com/world/2010/aug/15/france-haiti-independence-debt

[106] *The 11 Components of the French Colonial Tax in Africa,* Dr. Y, May 1, 2017, *Afro Legends,* https://afrolegends.com/2017/05/01/the-11-components-of-the-french-colonial-tax-in-africa/ See also *France/Afrique : 14 African Countries Forced by France to Pay Colonial Tax For the Benefits of Slavery and Colonization,* January 30, 2014, MediaPart https://blogs.mediapart.fr/jecmaus/blog/300114/franceafrique-14-african-countries-forced-france-pay-colonial-tax-benefits-slavery-and-colonization and *Italian deputy PM calls on EU to sanction France for its 'continued colonization' of Africa,* January 21, 2019, RT, https://www.rt.com/news/449303-france-africa-sanctions-colonializm/ see also *Italy Accuses*

France of Impoverishing Africa, Henry Ridgwell, January 23, 2019, VOA News, https://www.voanews.com/europe/italy-accuses-france-impoverishing-africa see also *China vs France: Battle for Africa?* – VisualPolitik, June 20, 2018, YouTube video, https://www.youtube.com/watch?v=rY8pCRSBd_o see also *How France loots its former colonies,* January 24, 2013, *This is Africa,* https://thisisafrica.me/politics-and-society/france-loots-former-colonies/ see also *French Colonialism Must End,* Senator Jim Inhofe, YouTube video https://www.youtube.com/watch?v=BFwpkiKPoUs&t=2s

[107] *Shadow War in the Sahara, 'War on terror' or competition for natural resources?* A look at the US and French military presence in Africa, May 13, 2017, Aljazeera, https://www.aljazeera.com/programmes/specialseries/2016/10/shadow-war-sahara-161009025023817.html see also *Mali, France and the war on terror in Africa, Horace Campbell, February 20, 2013,* Pambazuka News, https://www.pambazuka.org/human-security/mali-france-and-war-terror-africa see also *Tomgram: Nick Turse, America's Empire of African Bases, Nick Turse,* November 17, 2015, TomDispatch.com, http://www.tomdispatch.com/blog/176070/tomgram%3A_nick_turse,_america%27s_empire_of_african_bases/ see also *Africom's Secret Empire: US Military Turns Africa Into 'Laboratory' Of Modern Warfare,* December 11, 2015, Mint Press News, https://www.mintpressnews.com/211971-2/211971/

[108] *Landlocked Countries: Higher Transport Costs, Delays, Less Trade,* June 16, 2008, The World Bank, https://www.worldbank.org/en/news/feature/2008/06/16/landlocked-countries-higher-transport-costs-delays-less-trade and *The economics of landlocked countries,* The Economist, https://www.economist.com/the-americas/2015/05/09/interiors see also *The Economic Struggles of Landlocked Countries,* Jacob Goldberg, August 8, 2018, *Thought Co,* https://www.thoughtco.com/economic-struggles-of-landlocked-countries-1434532

[109] *Charity finds that US food aid for Africa hurts instead of helps,* Celia W. Dugger, August 14, 2007, *The New York Times,* https://www.nytimes.com/2007/08/14/world/americas/14iht-food.4.7116855.html see also *Myth 6: Africa needs our help,* Global Justice Now, https://www.globaljustice.org.uk/myth-6-africa-needs-our-help "*For decades, the dominant image of Africa has been that it is poor and helpless. This image is wrong. Most people in Africa may be poor, but the continent itself is one of the richest in terms of natural resources. Far from being helpless and dependent on our help, Africa pays more money to rich countries than it receives in aid. We need to face up to the uncomfortable truth: Africa is aiding us.*" See also *Trump's "trade war" includes punishing Africans for refusing second-hand American clothes,* Abdi Latif Dahir, Yomi Kazeem, April 5, 2018, *Quartz Africa,* https://qz.com/africa/1245015/trump-trade-war-us-suspends-rwanda-agoa-eligibility-over-secondhand-clothes-ban/ see also *Poverty Inc,* Documentary, 2014. The documentary discusses the "poverty industrial complex" that involves private corporations taking over social services for profit. See *When Poverty is Profitable,* Gillian B. White, *The Atlantic,* June 22, 2016, https://www.theatlantic.com/business/archive/2016/06/poverty-industry/487958/

[110] *Line in the sand crossed as Zimbabwe reaches a deal with evicted farmers,* Peta Thornycroft, *The Telegraph,* July 7, 2020, Yahoo News https://www.yahoo.com/news/line-sand-crossed-zimbabwe-reaches-170959067.html see also *Zimbabwe agrees to pay $3.5 billion dollars compensation to*

white farmers, July 29, 2020, *Reuters,* https://www.yahoo.com/news/zimbabwe-agrees-pay-3-5-112210112.html

[111] *Leopold II,* Adam Hochschild, June 9, 2020, *Britannica Encyclopedia,* https://www.britannica.com/biography/Leopold-II-king-of-Belgium

[112] Congo: Belgian, French & US Troops establish bases in Brazzaville, July 21, 2015, AP Archive, YouTube video https://www.youtube.com/watch?v=fFUVxEeWwDI

[113] Congo Investigates UN Driver for Trafficking Minerals, August 23, 2011, VOA News, https://www.voanews.com/africa/congo-investigates-un-driver-trafficking-minerals see also The UN caught stealing minerals in the Congo, September 24, 2019, Lip Stick Alley https://www.lipstickalley.com/threads/the-un-caught-stealing-minerals-in-the-congo.2799596/ see also *Gold worth billions smuggled out of Africa,* David Lewis, Ryan McNeill, Zandi Shabalala, April 23, 2019, *Reuters,* https://www.reuters.com/article/us-gold-africa-smuggling-exclusive/exclusive-gold-worth-billions-smuggled-out-of-africa-idUSKCN1S00IT The UAE received over $15 billion in gold, most of it stolen from African nations. See also *UN peacekeepers in Congo hold record for rape, sex abuse,* Krista Larson, Paisley Dodds, September 23, 2017, AP News, https://apnews.com/69e56ab46cab400f9f4b3753bd79c930/UN-peacekeepers-in-Congo-hold-record-for-rape,-sex-abuse see *also U.N. fails to stem rapes by peacekeepers in Africa, victims cry,* Christian Locka and Jabeen Bhatti, January 16, 2018, USA Today, https://www.usatoday.com/story/news/world/2018/01/16/u-n-fails-stem-rapes-peacekeepers-africa-victims-cry/1016223001/ in one instance a teenager was raped while a U.N. delegation was visiting the base she was rape at! See also *UN Peacekeeping has a Sexual Abuse Problem,* Skye Wheeler, January 11, 2020, *Human Rights Watch,* https://www.hrw.org/news/2020/01/11/un-peacekeeping-has-sexual-abuse-problem

[114] Life expectancy is about 60 years, World Health Organization, https://www.who.int/countries/cod/en/ see also *How Europe Underdeveloped Africa,* Walter Rodney, 1973, http://abahlali.org/files/3295358-walter-rodney.pdf see also *Belgium-Moving From Regret to Reparations,* Carine Dikiefu Banona and Jean-Sebasien Sepulchre, June 30, 2020, https://www.hrw.org/news/ 2020/06/30/belgium-moving-regrets-reparations see also *How Sub-Saharan Africans Contribute to the American economy,* January 2018, http://research .newamericaneconomy.org/wp-content/uploads/sites/2/2018/01/NAE_African_V6.pdf

[115] William H. Grier, Psychiatrist Who Delved into 'Black Rage' in 1960s, Dies at 89, Williams Grimes, September 11, 2015, New York Times

[116] *Legacy of Trauma, Context of the African American Experience,* Brandon Jones, https://www.health.state.mn.us/communities/equity/projects/infantmortality/session2.2.pdf

[117] Ibid

[118] Greatness is in Our DNA: From Being Worshipped Like Gods to Victims of Post Traumatic Slave Syndrome, Volume III, page 457, Dr. Rufus O. Jimerson, January 6, 2017 see also Genetic impact of African slave trade revealed in DNA study, July 24, 2020, BBC, Yahoo, https://www.yahoo.com/news/genetic-impact-colonial-era-slave-134523651.html

[119] *The Rape of Recy Taylor explores the little-known terror campaign against Black women,* Soraya Nadia Mcdonald, December 14, 2017, *The Undefeated,* https://theundefeated.com/features/the-rape-of-recy-taylor-explores-the-little-known-terror-campaign-against-black-women/

[120] Young Black kids are rehearsing lyrics about shooting "niggas" by ten years of age. *See Elementary School Boy Goes Off During Freestyle In His Room! "My Nxqqas Pulling Up And We Not Driving,"* February 20, 2020. World Star Hip Hop, https://www.worldstarhiphop.com/videos/video.php?v=wshh2cW4109msmfB26iG see also https://www.worldstarhiphop.com/videos/video.php?v=wshh0BXpjR12tF8kGmSf this video shows very young kids targeted with vile rap music.

[121] *Gang Members Implicate U.S. Government in Dumping Crates of Guns in Chicago,* Isaac Davis, September 13, 2016, Waking Times, https://www.wakingtimes.com/2016/09/13/gang-members-implicate-u-s-govt-dumping-crates-guns-chicago/ Once again white power thinks there needs to be a video recording of their dirty tricks. The most obvious indication that guns are intentionally put in Black areas is the amount of automatic machine guns that appeared in Black neighborhoods immediately after the introduction of crack-cocaine. The Black community asked out loud, "Where are all of these machine guns coming from?" The combination of crack *and machine guns* made government involvement blaringly obvious. Gang members in several cities have reported caches of guns being left in gang-infested neighborhoods. The U.S. has an extensive track record of gun-running and insiders blew the whistle on America arming ISIS and the publicized gun smuggling operation in Mexico known as Fast and Furious. See *El Chapo's Capture Puts 'Operation Fast and Furious' Back in the Headlines,* Ian Tuttle, January 22, 2016, *National Review,* https://www.nationalreview.com/2016/01/fast-furious-obama-first-scandal/ see also *Matt Drudge: 'America has been arming ISIS,'* Douglas Ernst, November 24, 2015, *WND,* https://www.wnd.com/2015/11/drudge-america-has-been-arming-isis/ The BBC News aired a documentary on the violence in Chicago and gang members admitted stockpiles of fully automatic guns are mysteriously left for them in allies, unlocked cars and back streets. Hundreds of gang members can't legally buy automatic guns so where are they getting them? *The Lost Streets of Chicago,* BBC News, September 7, 2016, https://www.bbc.com/news/video_and_audio/features/magazine-37292306/37292306

[122] *The Cold War Origin of the Model Minority Myth,* writer Frank Chin expressed it this way, "Whites love us because we are not Black!" See http://pzacad.pitzer.edu/~mma/teaching/MS80/readings/lee.pdf and *The Asian American Response to Black Lives Matter is Part of a Long, Complicated History,* Cady Lang, *Time,* June 26, 2020, *Yahoo News,* https://www.yahoo.com/news/asian-american-response-black-lives-184953852.html

[123] *Data shows Nigerians the most educated in the U.S.* January 12, 2018, Leslie Casimir, *Houston Chronicle,* https://www.chron.com/news/article/Data-show-Nigerians-the-most-educated-in-the-U-S-1600808.php see also Are Nigerian immigrants top of the class in the US? March 25, 2018, Africa Check, https://africacheck.org/reports/nigerian-immigrants-top-class-us/

[124] National Center for Education Statistics, Fast Facts, https://nces.ed.gov/fastfacts/display.asp?id=72 Lead poisoning also causes learning disabilities

and Blacks suffer from lead poisoning more than any other group, see *Childhood Lead Poisoning,* CDC, https://www.cdc.gov/nceh/lead/factsheets/Lead_fact_sheet.pdf#:~:text=Lead%20poisoning%20can%20affect%20nearly%20every%20system%20in,No%20safe%20blood%20lead%20level%20has%20been%20identified. See also At-Risk *Populations, CDC,* https://www.cdc.gov/nceh/lead/prevention/populations.htm

[125] *Intelligence Quotient (IQ), Emotional Quotient (EQ), and Spiritual Quotient (SQ). The power of self realization,* Jumanne Rajabu Mtambalike, March 4, 2017, *Medium,* https://medium.com/@jumannerajabumtambalike/intelligence-quotient-iq-emotional-quotient-eq-and-spiritual-quotient-sq-c4907f38dd95

[126] *The US is on the verge of a devastating, but avoidable doctor shortage,* Kunal Sindhu, July 30, 2019, *Quartz,* https://qz.com/1676207/the-us-is-on-the-verge-of-a-devastating-doctor-shortage/ see also *Donald Trump says African Americans built this nation!* October 6, 2019, *World Star Hip Hop,* https://www.worldstarhiphop.com/videos/video.php?v=wshhR43Sz2De701Jg6X8

[127] *In 1825 Haiti paid France $21 Billion To Preserve Its Independence—Time for France to Pay it Back,* Dan Sperling, December 6, 2017, Forbes, https://www.forbes.com/sites/realspin/2017/12/06/in-1825-haiti-gained-independence-from-france-for-21-billion-its-time-for-france-to-pay-it-back/#1311a384312b

[128] *The True Story Of The 1980s, When Everyone Was Convinced Japan Would Buy America,* Rob Wile, September 5, 2014, Business Insider http://www.businessinsider.com/japans-eighties-america-buying-spree-2014-9#so-in-september-1985-the-g-5-countries-signed-the-plaza-accord-the-non-american-ones-pledged-more-liberal-trade-policies-to-try-to-close-it-7 see also *Why did America rebuild the Japanese economy after World War II* https://www.gvsd.org/cms/lib02/PA01001045/Centricity/Domain/610/Why%20did%20the%20US%20rebuild%20Japan%20Wooksheet%201.pdf The US spent one million dollars a day for seven years to rebuild Japan, a figure that if adjusted for inflation would be astronomical today. See also *Occupation and Reconstruction of Japan,* 1945-52 https://history.state.gov/milestones/1945-1952/japan-reconstruction see also *The Destruction and Reconstruction of N. Korea,* Charles K. Armstrong, March 15, 2009 https://apjjf.org/-Charles-K.-Armstrong/3460/article.html see also *Singapore's 50 year relationship with US to be celebrated at White House state dinner,* Aza Wee Sile, August 1, 2016, CNBC https://www.cnbc.com/2016/08/01/singapores-50-year-relationship-with-us-to-be-celebrated-at-white-house-state-dinner.html See also *Trade in goods with Singapore,* U.S. Census, https://www.census.gov/foreign-trade/balance/c5590.html

[129] *In 'Cancer Alley,' a renewed focus on systemic racism is too late,* Luke Denne, June 21, 2020, NBC News, https://www.nbcnews.com/science/science-news/cancer-alley-renewed-focus-systemic-racism-too-late-n1231602) see also *The crisis in Flint goes deeper than water,* Evan Osnos, January 20, 2016, *The New Yorker,* https://www.newyorker.com/news/news-desk/the-crisis-in-flint-goes-deeper-than-the-water

[130] NYC *Nurse Has A Breakdown: Blows The Whistle On Doctors Forcing Deaths At Her Hospital Due To Coronavirus!* May 5, 2020, *World Star Hip Hop,*

https://www.worldstarhiphop.com/videos/video.php?v=wshhuHto7LDAln07ooPI

[131] *1951: We Charge Genocide*, July 15, 2011, *BlackPast*, https://www.blackpast.org/global-african-history/primary-documents-global-african-history/we-charge-genocide-historic-petition-united-nations-relief-crime-united-states-government-against/ see also *"We Charge Genocide," The 1951 Black Lives Matter Campaign*, Susan A. Glenn, University of Washington, https://depts.washington.edu/moves/CRC_genocide.shtml

[132] A Brief History of NBUF, Dr. Conrad W. Worrill, Founder of The National Black United Front, http://www.drconradworrill.com/abriefhistoryofn.html see also Cultural Genocide-Stripped of Racial and Cultural Identity, William E. Brown, Poor Magazine, https://www.poormagazine.org/node/5933

[133] *You have no friends*, Dr. John Henrik Clarke, Russell Jones channel, YouTube video https://www.youtube.com/watch?v=EnJtYDNIui8&t=6s

[134] Nazi Propaganda, United States Holocaust Memorial Museum, https://encyclopedia.ushmm.org/content/en/article/nazi-propaganda

[135] *3 Billion and Counting*, Documentary, 2010, Dr. Rutledge, watch for free at https://vimeo.com/158624102 and https://tubitv.com/movies/286006/3_billion_and_counting?utm_source=google-feed&tracking=google-feed

[136] The American Directory of Certified Uncle Toms page 42-43

Made in the USA
Monee, IL
12 February 2024

53427253R00105